PEABODY
MUSEUM
COLLECTIONS
SERIES

The Moche of Ancient Peru

THE MOCHE OF ANCIENT PERU

Media and Messages

Jeffrey Quilter

Foreword by Luis Jaime Castillo B.

Photographs by Mark Craig

Rubie Watson, Series Editor

Peabody Museum Press, Harvard University
CAMBRIDGE, MASSACHUSETTS

Editorial direction by Joan K. O'Donnell
Copy editing by Jane Kepp
Cover design by Kristina Kachele and Joan K. O'Donnell
Text design and composition by Kristina Kachele Design, llc
Production management by Kristina Kachele Design, llc
Proofreading by Donna Dickerson
Prepress by FCI Digital
Printed and bound in China at Everbest Printing Co. Ltd., through Four Colour Print Group

isbn 978-0-87365-406-7

Library of Congress Cataloging-in-Publication Data:
Quilter, Jeffrey, 1949-
The Moche of ancient Peru : media and messages / Jeffrey Quilter ; foreword by Luis Jaime Castillo B.; photographs by Mark Craig.
p. cm. — (Peabody Museum collections series)
Includes bibliographical references.
isbn 978-0-87365-406-7 (pbk. : alk. paper)
1. Mochica Indians. 2. Mochica Indians—Antiquities. 3. Mochica Indians—Antiquities—Catalogs. 4. Mochica pottery. 5. Mochica pottery—Catalogs. 6. Peabody Museum of Archaeology and Ethnology—Catalogs. I. Peabody Museum of Archaeology and Ethnology. II. Title.
f3430.1.m6q45 2010
985'.01—dc22
                    2010017348

This book is printed on acid-free paper.

Peabody Museum Press
11 Divinity Avenue
Cambridge, MA 02138, U.S.A.
www.peabody.harvard.edu/publications/

frontispiece: For seven centuries the people of the north coast of Peru participated in what has come to be called the Moche Archaeological Culture. Moche is best known for remarkable ceramics that depicted gods, heroes, and, apparently, ordinary people—as shown in this group photograph. Top row, left to right: PM 46-77-30/5031, 46-77-30/5088, 46-77-30/5065; middle row, l–r: 09-3-30/75622.5, 46-77-30/4961, 09-3-30/75631, 09-3-30/75614; bottom row, l–r: 09-3-30/75604.2, 46-77-30/4967, 09-3-30/75622. 98060003. J. David Bohl, photographer. Copyright © 2005 by the President and Fellows of Harvard College.

front and back covers: Front and rear views of Moche Phase IV portrait head stirrup-spout vessel from the Virú or Chicama Valley. PM 16-62-30/F729. Front: 98750073; back: 98720052. Mark Craig, photographer. Copyright © by the President and Fellows of Harvard College.

Contents

Illustrations

PLATES

Detail of the Maritime Frieze at Huaca Cao Viejo, Chicama Valley, Peru. Photo by Hal Starratt.

THE CHANGING WORLD OF MOCHE ARCHAEOLOGY

Luis Jaime Castillo B.

ARCHAEOLOGISTS HAVE LONG REGARDED the Peabody Museum's collection
of Moche artifacts as one of the finest in the world. Beginning with a contribution of
materials by Julio C. Tello, one of the founders of Peruvian archaeology and a Harvard
alumnus, and enhanced by later additions from various scholars and donors, the collection includes many outstanding pieces, each deserving its own detailed analysis.
In the pages of this book, those acquainted with Moche research will immediately
recognize emblematic objects such as the portrait head vessels in plates 11 and 12 and
on the cover; the curing session presided over by an owl–healer in plate 20; or the
congregation of skeletons around a mummy bundle in plate 19. With this publication,
an important part of the Peabody's collection becomes available to the general public
for the first time—providing an opportunity to enjoy and ponder the meaning of these
enigmatic objects.

   Although archaeological dogma gives absolute primacy to objects found *in
situ*—that is, in original settings and excavated through a rigorous archaeological

procedure—it is also unquestionable that museum collections, often composed primarily of unprovenienced artifacts, contain information that can be essential to understanding ancient societies. Purists would like us to ignore artifacts that were not found and registered by trained excavators, but to do so would exclude some of the most compelling portrayals of Moche society—objects that could have been produced by no one but the Moche. The "unique object," a piece that has no copies or that portrays aspects of Moche life that can be seen nowhere else, can be admired and studied by scholars even as we condemn the way in which it was obtained. What we cannot do is ignore an artifact, particularly an exceptional one, for the way in which it was found. As archaeologists and museum curators, our responsibility is to preserve it for the future, not only assuring its integrity but also contextualizing it within the grand narratives of its original society. This catalog is a tribute to these types of artifacts: distinctive pieces that deserve detailed explanations, objects that beg to be considered from many angles and that are great creations of the human spirit. By themselves, however, the objects cannot accomplish the purpose of communicating who the Moche were and why their study inspires us.

In *The Moche of Ancient Peru*, Jeffrey Quilter presents the artifacts from the Peabody Museum collection—beautifully photographed and explained in great detail—wrapped in an account of the Moche that enlivens the objects and gives meaning to the society that produced them. Putting together this up-to-date narrative of the Moche, and of what archaeologists have figured out about them, has not been an easy task. An enormous amount of new information has emerged from the excavations on the north coast of Peru in the last twenty years, and readers are fortunate that this study was written by a scholar who has been at the forefront of this research.

During Quilter's academic lifespan, the Moche of northern Peru have become one of the most thoroughly researched and recognizable archaeological cultures of ancient South America, but they remain among the most complex, mysterious, and difficult societies to summarize in a single volume. Only a few years after the discovery in 1987 of the royal tombs at Sipán—the richest ancient burials yet found in the Western hemisphere—large-scale and long-lasting multidisciplinary research programs began at the Huaca de la Luna, Huaca Cao Viejo, and San José de Moro. These research programs were followed by many others ranging from research on specific sites to whole regions and from generic, society-level approaches to the examination of specific subjects such as paleoethnobotany, the genetic composition of populations, and the technology used to produce ceramics and metals.

Before 1987, when Walter Alva and his team of archaeologists excavated the first royal tomb at Sipán, Moche research was perceived as a fairly closed subject. It was widely thought that the excellent work led by Rafael Larco and followed by scholars like Christopher Donnan and Michael Moseley had revealed all that could be learned about this ancient people. Larco's chronology, based largely on a detailed study of his collections, now housed in the Rafael Larco Herrera Museum in Lima, was widely confirmed, as were his ideas about Moche religion and ritual life. For much of the 1960s, '70s, and '80s, work had focused on the interpretation of Moche's rich iconographic record, revealing its structure and function—including Jeffrey Quilter's original work on the narrative structure of Moche iconography. But events unfolding in Sipán were to demonstrate that the facts of Moche life were far from settled.

No *mochicologo* (a student of the Moche) expected in the mid-1980s that a royal burial would be excavated in his or her lifetime. The largest Moche burial found to that point had been that of the Warrior-Priest of Huaca de la Cruz, excavated by William Duncan Strong and Clifford Evans in the late 1940s as part of the Virú Valley Project led by Harvard's Gordon R. Willey. It was assumed that all other burials must already have been looted, many by early Spanish settlers. But when royal and high-elite burials appeared at Sipán, La Mina, San José de Moro, Huaca de la Luna, Huaca Cao, and Úcupe, we realized that the Moche were much more highly developed than originally thought. The conditions revealed by empirical archaeological data about technological advancement, social organization, political configuration, and artistic tradition proved to be more complex than anything previously imagined by Peruvianist archaeologists.

These research programs have resulted in hundreds of scholarly publications based on the extraordinary material manifestations of Moche achievements, including large research collections of artifacts with numerous museum-quality pieces; royal, elite, and commoner burials; and large temples decorated with polychrome designs.

Rather than making the Moche more comprehensible, this wealth of information and materials—ably described and analyzed in this volume—has ironically created a high level of confusion about this ancient society and reminds us that often in archaeology, the more we know of a phenomenon, the less we understand it.

Jeffrey Quilter's concise and provocative book on the Peabody Museum's Moche collection approaches the Moche through the lens of an anthropological archaeologist interested in understanding the social and cultural processes that shaped this unique society. Luckily for the reader, it also indulges the fascination provoked by the exceptional artistic qualities of Moche material culture. Quilter's intimate relationship with the Moche—an enduring affair that has led him to explore many different manifestations of Moche society—is expressed in this book's passionate and deliberately subjective account of a research subject in constant flux. Even as we write these pages, new excavations and new insights are contributing new information. *The Moche of Ancient Peru* more than fulfills its mission of introducing and illustrating some of the most fascinating archaeological investigations currently being undertaken in the New World.

ACKNOWLEDGMENTS

MANY PEOPLE HELPED bring this book into being. I thank William L. Fash, director of the Peabody Museum, for initiating the idea that I curate the exhibit from which the book was developed, and Rebecca Chetham, then deputy director, for helping with the finances to make it happen. Thanks also to the many staff members of the Peabody Museum who helped make the exhibit a reality, particularly Samuel Tager, Nynke Dorhout Jolly, Genevieve Fisher, and Pamela Gerardi.

For this book, I especially thank Joan K. O'Donnell, Donna Dickerson, and the members of the Publications Committee of the Peabody Museum. The staff of the museum's Collections Department was helpful in many stages of working with the Moche collection, for both the exhibit and the book. Many are to be thanked, but I offer my special appreciation to Steven LeBlanc, director of collections, David DeBono Schafer, senior collections manager, and Susan Haskell, curatorial associate for special projects. Thanks also to Mark Craig, who took the beautiful photographs for the plates in this book.

I greatly appreciate the help of Richard L. Burger, Adam Herring, and Allan Maca, pre-Columbianist colleagues who read drafts of the book and offered useful advice and comments, as did Sarah Quilter, who offered many valuable insights into ways to make the book better. Michel Conan, director of Garden History and Landscape Studies while I was at Dumbarton Oaks (DO), offered me much to consider regarding art and culture, and Joanne Pillsbury, my successor in Pre-Columbian Studies at DO, always offers important and stimulating insights whenever I talk to her. Christopher Donnan was extremely helpful in commenting and offering advice on various aspects of Moche style.

Harvard graduate students Michele Koons and Lisa Trever offered insights through many conversations, as did Yale graduate student Oscar Gabriel Prieto. Undergraduate and graduate students alike helped me to clarify my thoughts in my seminar "The Moche of Ancient Peru: Politics, Economy, Religion, and Art," offered at Harvard University in the spring term of 2009 and in another version in spring of 2010.

Donald McClelland was generous in allowing me to use the fine renderings of Moche art made by his late wife, Donna. A number of other colleagues, friends, and institutions also lent the products of their talents, particularly Santiago Uceda and Ricardo Morales, directors of the Huaca de la Luna Project, Ándres Álvarez Calderón Larco, executive director of the Museo Rafael Larco Herrera, curator Ulla Homquist of the same institution, and photographer Ira Block.

Special thanks also to the Fundación Wiese of Lima, Peru, which has supported my work, and to Marco Aveggio of that institution, who has been so gracious and generous in aiding me. The directors of the El Brujo archaeological project, Regulo Franco, César Gálvez, and Segundo Vásquez, are also greatly thanked for a multitude of favors and support. I am grateful in particular to Luis Jaime Castillo, who has helped me in innumerable ways to conduct research in Peru and from whom I have learned much. Thanks also to the National Institute of Culture of Peru, especially its branch office in Trujillo.

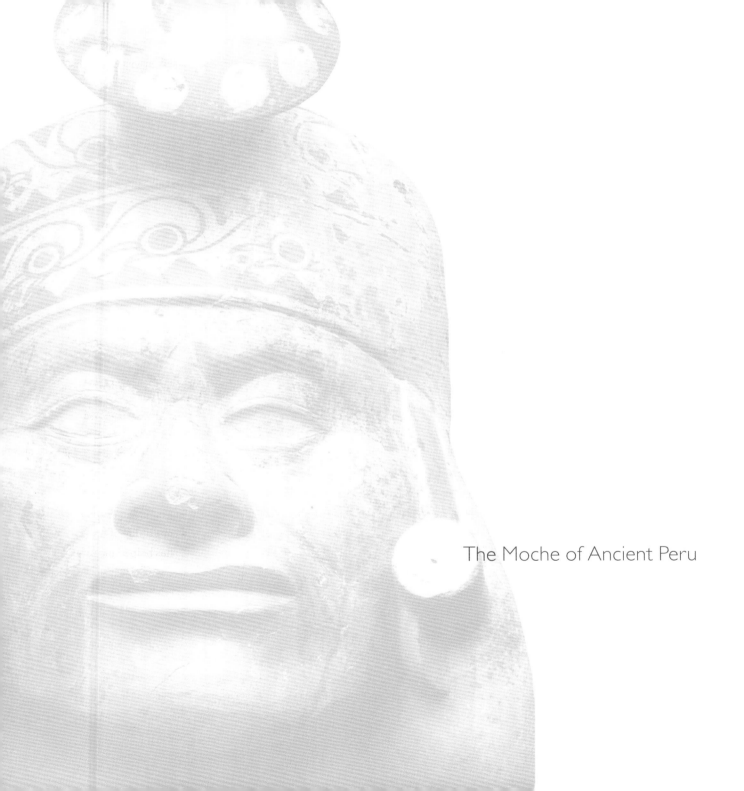

The Moche of Ancient Peru

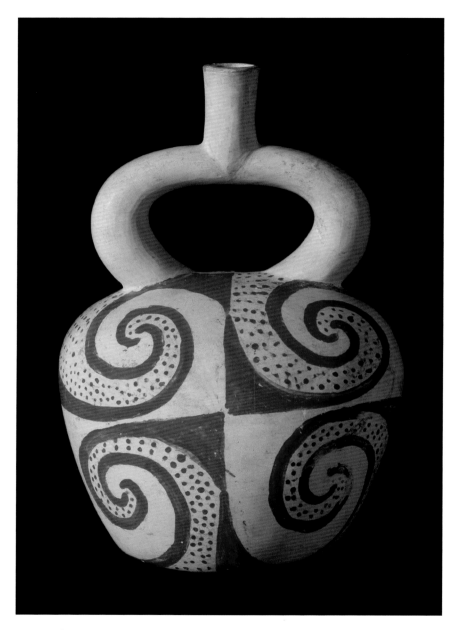

Early Moche stirrup-spout vessel. The volutes in the painted design might refer to ocean waves or the tentacles of an octopus. The design typifies Moche artists' delight in playing with positive and negative spaces that express opposed but complimentary forces or things. PM 09-3-30/75626.9 (W 17 × H 21.5 cm). 98540019. Mark Craig, photographer.

Introduction

PERU'S NORTH COAST is a barren strip of desert fronting one of the world's richest maritime habitats, a bountiful fishery created by the cold waters of the Humboldt, or Peru, Current. Inland the desert gives way to mountains and plateaus of the Andes, dissected by rivers running roughly parallel to one another from east to west and debouching onto the coastal strip. From remote antiquity until today, well-engineered irrigation systems drawing on these rivers have nurtured vast green fields of maize, beans, and squash in the valley bottoms. The cornucopia of food provided by the ocean and the valleys supported a sequence of complex human societies beginning in very early times. One of the most spectacular of these ancient cultures, dating from about A.D. 100 to 800—in European terms, from the time of the early Roman Empire to the reign of Charlemagne—is known as Moche.

On the summits of dazzlingly painted, adobe-brick temple complexes, Moche priests and priestesses once stood resplendent in elaborate costumes of gold, precious stones, textiles, and feathers. Presenting themselves as gods to crowds of

The Virú Valley, looking upstream. The small stream in the foreground is a result of the siphoning of water by irrigation canals. The Andes can be seen in the distance. Photo by the author.

onlookers gathered in plazas below, they watched as warriors armed with shields and clubs, spear throwers and slings paraded captured prisoners to be sacrificed.

Priests and warriors occupied the highest ranks of Moche society, ruling over members of the lower classes, who tilled the fields and produced the elaborate para-phernalia for rituals and war. Next to the largest temples stood cities with streets and avenues along which lay residential compounds. Within them and at specialized workshops, artisans produced some of the most beautiful metal objects found in the New World. Others created one of the Americas' most distinctive ceramic traditions (pl. 1). The works of these craftspeople were used in rituals, served as status symbols among the living, and entered the tombs of both low- and high-ranking Moche to accompany them in the afterlife.

Today, in museums throughout the world, Moche ceramics commonly capture the attention of visitors. The Moche's representational art style, depicting gods, priests, warriors, animals, plants (pl. 4), and seemingly the full spectrum of everyday life, appeals strongly to modern tastes and sensibilities. It is primarily through these ceramics and the personages and scenes painted and modeled on them that scholars have attempted, for more than a century, to understand the ancient Moche.

The appeal of Moche ceramics, together with the lure of the gold that lies buried in Moche ruins, has also had unfortunate consequences. Ever since Spaniards arrived on the north coast of Peru in the 1530s, people have been pillaging Moche temples, burials, and other ancient sites for their wealth. Many archaeological sites in Peru are so pockmarked with looters' holes that they look like the surface of the moon. Until after World War II, most of the looting was for gold. Collecting pottery in the wake of looters often became, ironically, a form of "salvage" archaeology. Many important museum collections, both in Peru and abroad, were built through this practice or through "excavation" using standards that would be unacceptable today. Even so, such museum collections, consisting of artifacts lacking detailed information about archaeological context—or provenience, as it is known in archaeology—can still aid scholarship and inform the public through exhibits and publications.

The great number of poorly documented ceramics and other artifacts in museums in Peru and around the world has created a peculiar situation for understanding the Moche.

Looting of Peruvian archaeological sites was celebrated in popular literature in the nineteenth century. In this illustration from *The Gold Fish of the Gran Chimu,* by Charles F. Lummis (1895), hard-working looters defend their "rights" against a proposed law banning excavations in the "mummy mines."

Craters of a moonlike landscape at the El Brujo archaeological complex, in the Chicama Valley, bearing witness to centuries of looting. Looting has stopped at this site but continues elsewhere. Photo by the author.

We know a great deal about certain aspects of the ceramics—how they were made, how they were decorated, and how styles changed over time—yet great gaps exist in our knowledge. As just one example, until recently we have had only rudimentary knowledge of regional variations in the Moche style, because so many pots lack identification even of the valleys where they were found. Furthermore, although study of the images molded or painted on ceramics allows scholars to make reasonable inferences about Moche religion, warfare, economics, and other aspects of life, a dearth of archaeological evidence has meant that theories derived from studies of ceramics and other unprovenienced artifacts could not be tested with independent data. Happily, this situation is changing as the results of recent field archaeology begin to be published. Archaeologists are providing valuable information about ceramics found in tombs, houses, workshops, and other locales. They offer carefully pieced-together views of political organization and other aspects of the people and societies that produced these artistic masterworks.

The Peabody Museum of Archaeology and Ethnology at Harvard University houses an impressive collection of Moche artifacts. These objects, especially the ceramic vessels that make up the greatest part of the collection, were media that conveyed messages about the way people thought about themselves, their gods, and their places in the universe. Because of the richness of the collection, it became the subject of an exhibition I was asked to organize for the Peabody Museum. Titled *The Moche of Ancient Peru: Media and Messages,* it ran from October 2005 to January 2008. In this book I discuss many of the artifacts shown in the exhibition and present archaeologists' latest thinking about Moche society.

View of the Huacas de Moche site, in the lower Moche Valley, from the summit of Huaca de la Luna looking west to Huaca del Sol. The urban sector lies between the two in the valley bottom. Some excavated residential units are visible in the middle distance. Photo by the author.

MOCHE AND ITS ART STYLE

THE NAME "MOCHE" comes from the Moche Valley, the location of two large, prehistoric adobe structures known in Spanish as the Huacas de Moche—loosely translated as "the Temples of Moche." It was there that the first archaeological excavations of Moche artifacts took place in the late nineteenth century. The name for the valley and the site likely derived from the word "Muchik," the name of a language spoken on the north coast of Peru at the time Spaniards arrived there in 1532. It survived until sometime in the eighteenth century. Some archaeologists use the term "Mochica," also derived from the name for the language, to refer to the same archaeological phenomenon. This term emphasizes the long continuities that many archaeologists see on the north coast, although we do not know what language or languages the Moche spoke. Many archaeologists use "Moche" and "Mochica" interchangeably, and generally scholars place no great import on one term over the other.[1] Another convenient name for the north coast area where the Moche art style and associated cultural practices predominated is "Mochilandia."

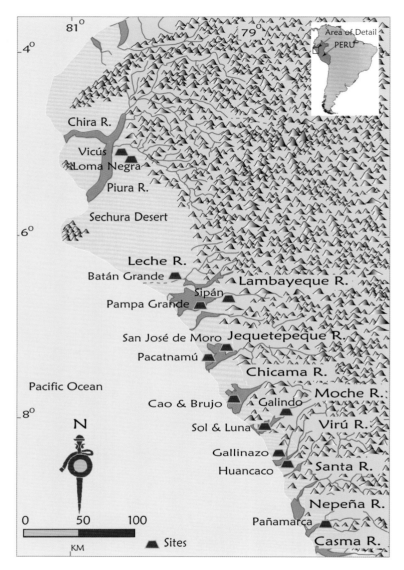

The north coast of Peru, showing principal Moche archaeological sites. Many more than these exist. Map by the author.

Details of the origins and demise of the Moche style are unclear and are currently being investigated. Researchers commonly think of the Moche Valley and neighboring Chicama Valley as the Moche heartland, but variants of the art style were eventually made as far north as the Chira Valley and as far south as the Nepeña Valley.

Among the art styles of ancient South America, the Moche tradition has received much attention because of its use of a representational mode that seems "readable" to modern people, depicting plants, animals, and personages. Although other pre-Columbian cultures, especially those to the north, employed "realistic" representations in their art, Moche artists were exceptional in the degree to which they used this style, the length of time over which they developed and elaborated it, and the range of subject matter they covered.

Although Moche art initially seems very approachable, once past a superficial engagement the viewer faces many challenges in interpreting it. Why, for example, is a spiny shell depicted as a ceramic vessel? Are the personages shown in this battle scene gods or mortals? Is the ceremony depicted one that actually took place or a reference to some kind of celestial get-together among the gods? Over the years, scholars have offered varied views on such issues, and even today, interpretations differ considerably.

As Maya archaeologist Simon Martin has observed, the Moche mode of artistic representation provides an easy, "entry-level" means of reading the code presented by the images.[2] Comprehending the "texts" expressed in such a code usually requires extra information, beyond the images themselves. In a comparable example, a Christian who knows the story of the birth of Jesus is able fairly easily to interpret Christmas cards and imagery such as sculptured crèches. For some art styles, written texts can provide these sorts of external references. We have no such references for Moche, which, like the other ancient South American cultures, had no writing.

The very fact that one can discuss Moche or any other art style using the analogy of texts is significant, because this is only one of many ways in which art may be interpreted. For example, some works of art, such as large, repeating, iconic images of the faces of gods or geometric patterns across a wall, may reasonably be understood not as telling a story, the way texts do, but as designed to create an experience. This is the case with much of Moche art, especially mural art at temples. Nevertheless, many Moche images were made in reference to gods and heroes and to religious narratives about them—frequently, though not exclusively, on ceramics.

Lacking written records, our understandings and interpretations of the Moche are based mostly on archaeology and the study of the rich visual record ancient artists and craftspeople left in their creations, especially pottery. Several hundred years passed between the end of Moche society and the arrival of Spaniards with their quills, inks, and papers. The Spaniards occasionally wrote down local legends and stories as they attempted to document native beliefs so that they could extirpate paganism and convert natives to Christianity. The recording of legends in aid of eliminating them unwittingly ran counter to the Spaniards' aims, for such records now serve as testaments to pre-Hispanic beliefs. In addition, some cultural practices proved strong enough to last from Moche times into the early colonial period. Consequently, Spanish records of legends and other aspects of sixteenth-century life on the Peruvian north coast can be used, with care, to interpret the long-gone Moche.

Nose ornament, silver and gold alloy, depicting the deity called the Decapitator standing on a two-headed feline-serpent. The ornament was buried with the Señora de Cao, a high-status young woman at the site known as Huaca Cao Viejo. Courtesy Fundación Wiese.

Ancient Life on the North Coast

THE DRY DESERT OF THE PERUVIAN COAST preserved buried materials such as cloth, fibers, leather, wood, and gourds that elsewhere would have disintegrated in cycles of rain and aridity, heat and cold. But although the Peruvian desert is well known for its great preservative qualities, the north coast desert is not as dry as the south coast of Peru. Even today, showers occasionally fall on the desert during the South American autumn, March and April, and there may have been times in the centuries since Moche culture disappeared when brief rains were more common. These, as well as periodic heavy rains and floods brought on by disruptions in patterns of off-shore ocean currents—especially in the second half of the sixth century and into the seventh—likely drenched many artifacts and hastened their disintegration. Although archaeologists occasionally find organic materials such as textiles at Moche sites (pl. 10), these kinds of discoveries happen more often in other parts of coastal Peru.

The Moche art style developed at a time when most of the major domesticated plants and animals of the Andes had been under human control for many centuries.

So, too, mastery of critical irrigation technology was well established, as were skills in metallurgy, ceramics, architecture, and many other technologies. Moche culture, rather than being brought about by radically new technologies, appears to have emerged because of changing social and political relations. At the time, Moche rituals and art helped to create and maintain new social arrangements; seen in retrospect, the whole Moche phenomenon is the expression of those changes. In Moche times, the extent of irrigation systems appears to have grown dramatically, with a concurrent increase in population. The degree to which these shifts were related to the development of the religious system and the political arrangements that went with them are part of what scholars are currently investigating.

Moche metallurgy was quite advanced. Workers mined and smelted ores with great skill, and techniques for working the refined metal included casting as well as sheet work (pl. 9). Moche people used metal not primarily to make tools but to craft elaborate ornaments and jewelry for high-ranking priests and lords. Metalsmiths mixed copper and gold in varying proportions. Sometimes they dipped copper and gold alloy objects into an acid bath made from plants. The acid ate away the copper a few molecules deep on the object's surface, leaving a thin layer of pure gold that could be burnished to a high gloss. Materials scientist Heather Lechtmann has proposed that this technique of "depletion gilding" was done not solely to make an alloy look like pure gold, in the sense of making a "cheaper" object look more valuable—as might be done in Western mercantile societies. It might rather have ensured that the "essence" of gold was present throughout the entire object. Objects created from alloys would have been tougher and more durable than objects with a high gold content as well, although many of the jewelry items Lechtmann discusses did not require such durability. Moche ornaments were often thin, maximizing metal for its brilliant effect.[3]

Ancient Andean peoples based their economies not on money, on land as property, or, probably, on objects thought to have inherent value, such as gold, as is the case in contemporary Western societies. For the later Inca, we know that the most valuable gifts the emperor gave to men were wives.[4] More wives meant more children, and both enlarged the number of a man's followers. Similar principles likely operated in earlier times. The Inca also valued fine textiles and jewelry made from metals, rare shells, and semiprecious stones. The rarity of these items—exotic objects from afar—likely gave them worth, but so, equally, did their value as sources of condensed energy, especially light energy, and as tokens of social relations between givers and recipients.[5]

Moche farmers raised maize, beans, squashes, a great variety of fruits, and fine cotton for textiles in fields nurtured by long irrigation canals. People obtained meat by hunting in valley woodlands and hills and by fowling in lagoons, marshes, and estuaries. Abundant maritime resources, including fish, seabirds, and mollusks, were available to coastal dwellers, who could exchange dried or salted fish with people in inland communities. Winter fogs nurtured specialized plant communities, known as *lomas,* on the coastal hills. Some lomas were only patches of low herbaceous plants; others may have been small forests lasting for much of the year. Lomas supported deer as well as a variety of small animals. Snails are abundant in lomas and supplied a minor but savory food, high in protein, when the lomas were in bloom.

Probably only members of the highest-ranking classes hunted deer (pl. 5), as was the case in contemporary Europe. Deer remains are rare at Moche sites, 'and the animals might have been hunted more

Moche vessel in the *florero,* or "flower pot," style, decorated with monster snails. The vessel's crenellated rim might refer to the upper walls of temples, which Moche builders often embellished with such architectural details. PM 46-77-30/4928 (W 22 × H 9.5 cm). Top view: 98540075; side view 98540074. Mark Craig, photographer.

Moche jar depicting a deer hunt in a painted scene on the vessel's body and in sculpted figures that form the top of the vessel. The fine-line painting shows men throwing spears at deer trapped in nets. In both painting and modeled figures, the coup de grace is carried out with a club. PM 16-62-30/F726 (W 17 x H 23.8 cm). 98540051. Mark Craig, photographer.

for ritual purposes than for food. Guinea pigs and ducks (pl. 2) were domesticated and kept within easy reach for their meat. North coast people seem to have eaten llamas only when they were sacrificed at festivals or ceremonies, whereas domesticated guinea pigs more regularly provided small but reliable amounts of protein.

Llamas will refuse to carry human riders, spitting and kicking at anyone who attempts to mount them. But an adult llama can carry close to 100 pounds of freight, so the Moche used llamas as pack animals to haul great quantities of materials over long distances (pl. 3). The related alpaca provided fine wool for textiles, although alpacas were raised more easily in their highland natural habitats than on the coast. A local camelid, a *warizo*—a crossbreed between a llama and an alpaca—may have been raised on the coast, however.[6]

On land, everyone traveled by foot except for lords and ladies, who were carried in litters. Long-distance merchants traveled by sea on large balsa-wood rafts. In the sixteenth century, Spanish explorers reported that the largest rafts were powered by sails, and evidence suggests that they could tack against the wind. Such large rafts brought red-rimmed *Spondylus princeps* shells—spiny oysters—from the warm coastal waters of Ecuador to northern Peru. In Inca times, *Spondylus* shells were more precious than gold. Moche artisans used them in small quantities, although near the end of the Moche era, trade in the shells appears to have boomed. Fishermen used smaller craft than did merchants, fashioning them from *totora* reeds. Some such craft are still used today on the north coast of Peru, where they are known as *caballitos del mar,* or seahorses.

An aspect of life on the north coast of Peru that is critical for understanding Moche society is the importance of irrigation canals. These artificial rivers, carrying water to land beyond the floodplains, have a long history in ancient Peru. The social organization required to construct and, equally important, maintain such canals may be simple, but the accompanying potential for conflict over water rights is great, and the regularization of water distribution can be complicated. The degree to which social factors surrounding irrigation were involved in the development of Moche culture has yet to be fully explored.

In dry environments like coastal Peru, canals feed fields cleared in places otherwise beyond the reaches of rivers, greatly increasing the amount of food that farmers can produce. In a society in which the majority of people raised their own food and walking was the sole means of transportation, most Moche lived close to their fields. Ancient Peruvians tended to live on the slopes of unirrigated hills in order to leave the watered, fertile bottomlands available for growing crops. Complexes of important buildings such as temples—known by their name in the Quechua language, *huacas,* meaning something imbued with sacredness—tended to be located away from or on the edges of agricultural fields.[7] Most valleys in Mochilandia feature one major *huaca* complex and several smaller ones. Such sites, both residential and ceremonial, in valleys and between them, are only now beginning to be investigated.

Recent work also has shown that some of the big huaca sites were citylike complexes with blocks of residences separated by streets. Examples of such complexes are found between the two large structures at Huacas de Moche (see illustration on p. 8) and at the El Brujo archaeological complex in the Chicama Valley. Other citylike complexes appear at sites with no large huaca clearly present. One example is Mocollope, also in the Chicama Valley, which has structures with both large halls and smaller rooms clustered on and around a large hill in midvalley (see illustration on p. 78).

Many Moche canals now lie beneath later constructions. This photograph shows an aqueduct of the Ascope Canal built during the Chimú era, after the Moche period. It runs along the Chicama Valley for almost three-quarters of a mile. Photo by the author.

Archaeologists have not yet studied such sites in great detail, but they give the impression of being urban centers where a diversity of activities took place. They certainly played crucial roles in the political and economic lives of people in the north coast valleys, but what kinds of social and political systems were in operation are unclear.

Questions concerning the social fabric of the north coast, the degree of variability in people's social arrangements, and changes through time lie at the heart of anthropological archaeology in Peru. They are the reasons archaeologists study the ceramics, gold jewelry, and huacas. Before I address some of these questions, though, I want to look at conceptual frameworks for understanding the past, the history of studies that have led to current understandings of Moche society, and the nature of the artifacts that have served as the primary evidence on which these understandings have been built.

Bottle in the Cupisnique style, a predecessor of Moche style from the north coast Initial period. Cupisnique artisans favored highly polished surfaces, often with stylized designs. PM 968-14-30/8614 (W 15.5 x H 20.5 cm). 98540018. Mark Craig, photographer.

Moche in Andean Prehistory

MOCHE ARTISANS WERE THE INHERITORS of millennia of artistic and technological traditions. The Moche marshalled many existing practices and reworked them under new social arrangements and cultural norms. Just as the glories of the Classical Greek city–states rested upon the preceding Minoan and Mycenaean civilizations, so Moche was built on foundations laid by earlier cultures.[8]

Exactly when humans entered the American continents is still a matter of debate, but it can safely be said that they had arrived by 12,000 years ago, adapting to new environments as the last Ice Age waned. In the Andes, humans exploited the rich resources of sea and shore, the coastal valleys, and highland and tropical forests. Between 4,500 and 3,500 years ago, perhaps earlier in some places, people began to construct large buildings, usually of stone with some adobe bricks, grouped together in what archaeologists refer to as "ceremonial centers." During this first building phase, from about 2500 to 1500 B.C.—centuries before similar developments in Mesoamerica—people in Peru did not yet make ceramics or weave textiles using

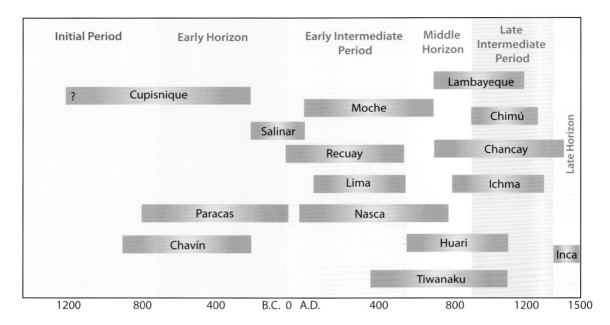

Approximate time spans of prehistoric Peruvian cultures mentioned in the text. The full time spans of the Initial Period and earlier are not shown. Illustration by the author.

a heddle loom. Archaeologists label this phase the Late Preceramic period. These ancient Peruvians, however, were already well along in domesticating plants. During the succeeding Initial period (about 1500–800 B.C.), people built even larger structures and adopted pottery and loom weaving. These crafts served as new media by which to express social identities, political associations, and religious convictions.

Late Preceramic and Initial period constructions were massive. Many early sites, such as Caral, have been found in the Supe Valley, on the coast not far north of Lima, and it is striking that in this area, as well as in valleys farther south, different architectural patterns and probably different ceremonial systems were already in existence. El Paraíso, for example, in the Chillón Valley on the central coast—on the northern edge of metropolitan Lima—consisted of seven or eight stone buildings spread across 58 hectares (143 acres). Two of the largest buildings each measured more than 300 meters (984 feet) long, paralleling each other and flanking a 7-hectare (17-acre)

Huari-style vessel in the form of a canteen. The bright colors and painting style were innovations that departed from earlier ceramic traditions on the north coast when ceramics like this were introduced. PM 46-77-30/5405 (W 15 x H 17 cm). 98540055. Mark Craig, photographer.

Exactly what happened at the end of the Moche era is uncertain. Some kinds of Huari influence came from that southern highland center to the religious center of Pachacamac, in the Lurín Valley. The nature of the takeover is unclear, but influences in the form of beautiful ceramics in styles of both the Huari heartland and Pachacamac began to appear in Mochilandia in the Middle Horizon. In the

A courtyard at Chan Chan, capital of the Chimor kingdom in the Moche Valley. The relatively low architecture with many large plazas suggests that Chimú people followed social, political, and religious practices different from those of Moche and earlier times. Photo by the author.

Jequetepeque Valley, research by Luis Jaime Castillo, of the Catholic University of Peru in Lima, and his team suggests that people from the highland region of Cajamarca to the east, after years of contact with the people of the lower valley, may have entered the region and taken over political power. Elsewhere, in the Moche Valley, the Huacas de Moche may have lost their prestige but continued to be occupied while a new citylike center, Galindo, was established farther up the valley.

Tiwanaku and Huari eventually collapsed like other archaeological cultures before them. As in earlier times, social unrest and instability may have lasted for a century or two before new systems emerged. The cultures of the Late Intermediate period (about A.D. 1000–1450)—represented on the north coast by Lambayeque and Chimú—still lingered in people's memories when the Spaniards arrived in 1532. At that time, the

Inca Empire had only recently conquered many of the Late Intermediate period societies. The Spaniards noted what they interpreted as political units or "nations" dominated by the Inca, such as the Chincha on the south coast, the Ichma on the central coast, and the kingdom of Chimor, the culture associated with Chimú archaeology, which had once covered an area on the north coast slightly larger than that previously influenced by the Moche. By 1532, Moche culture was many centuries gone, but the ruins of its temples dominated the landscape. People treated them as sacred places of the ancestors, places wrapped in legend and mystery.[14]

THE GREAT PYRAMID OF MOCHE.

The Great Pyramid of Moche, now known as Huaca del Sol, as rendered in Ephraim
George Squier's *Peru: Incidents of Travel and Exploration in the Land of the Incas* (1877).

A Brief History of Moche Studies

SPANIARDS OCCUPIED THE NORTH COAST of Peru early in the colonial period. Francisco Pizarro passed through the northern Moche region in 1532 on his way to meet and capture the Inca emperor in the highland city of Cajamarca. In 1534, the Spaniards returned when Diego de Almagro founded the city of Trujillo, naming it after the Spanish hometown of Pizarro, who made the founding official the following year. Trujillo sat between two ancient sites still venerated by native Peruvians at the time. To the south lay the great Huacas de Moche, consisting of Huaca del Sol and Huaca de la Luna, and to the north sprawled the vast, citylike Chimú architectural complex of Chan Chan. Although some of the early Spanish conquistadors, such as Cieza de León, wrote accounts of their own adventures or histories of the Inca, few members of the first waves of Spanish invaders took much interest in the past except as a source of wealth. Huaca del Sol, in the Moche Valley, was leased out for mining rights, and entrepreneurs diverted the Moche River to erode the huaca's adobe bricks, a form of "legal" vandalism that yielded a treasure in gold.

Spaniards also looted the great burial chambers of the lords of Chan Chan. They learned from the Inca that this great adobe complex of walled enclosures had been the capital city of a kingdom known as Chimor, a chief rival to the Inca less than a hundred years before the Spaniards arrived. Later in the colonial period, the archbishop of Trujillo, Martínez de Compañón, had elaborate illustrations made of parts of Chan Chan, Huaca del Sol, and other antiquities for a report on the natural and cultural history of the region that he prepared for Spain's King Carlos III.[15]

Swiss naturalist Johann Jakob von Tschudi joined forces with Peruvian Francisco de Rivero, traveling to sites and studying artifacts in ruins from the late 1830s through the 1840s. In 1851 the two published the first modern discussion of Peruvian antiquities, *Antigüedades peruanas.* The work concentrated on Inca sites and what the authors assumed to have been mostly Inca artifacts. The north coast lay outside the area they covered. The American diplomat–adventurer–scholar Ephraim George Squier, who had explored burial and temple mounds of the Ohio Valley, did travel through the north coast and reported on sites in his 1877 book, *Peru: Incidents of Travel and Exploration in the Land of the Incas.* It combined a travelogue with some superficial treatment of the ancient remains, but it is one of the few available accounts of its time in English that informed distant readers about an exotic, faraway land and its rich past.

Archaeology as we know it today did not become relatively standardized until the last half of the nineteenth century. In 1899, German archaeologist Max Uhle carried out the first archaeological project on the north coast, laying the foundations of professional archaeology in Peru. Uhle's work included important excavations at Huaca de la Luna, where he uncovered 37 graves on a platform next to the temple. Soon, other archaeologists, including Alfred Kroeber, an American, also investigated Huaca de la Luna, and gradually Moche archaeology emerged. But the long distances and slow pace of international travel impeded many foreign archaeologists from working in Peru until after World War II, and Peruvian national archaeology remained relatively small-scale.[16]

As research progressed, scholars began to identify the dark gray or black pottery commonly found at sites such as Chan Chan as "Chimú." Pottery of lighter color that

Rafael Larco Hoyle, at right, at a north coast community around 1925–1930. Besides his prodigious work in archaeology, Larco worked in ethnography, documenting traditional lifeways among rural people on his beloved north coast. Courtesy Museo Larco, Lima.

shared some motifs with the Chimú ceramics was quickly identified as earlier in date, and many researchers referred to it as "Proto-Chimú."

In the twentieth century, a local sugarcane plantation hacienda owner, Rafael Larco Hoyle, conducted research on Moche topics that established modern approaches to and understandings of the archaeological record. Larco's family hacienda was in the Chicama Valley, so he was raised in the midst of archaeological sites, and he often excavated on his own property. Educated in agronomy at Cornell University, he was an exceptionally gifted and conscientious avocational archaeologist, working mostly from the 1930s through the early 1960s. Although self-trained, he made careful notes, drawings, and photographs of his excavations and published the results quickly and at high standards for his day. It was Larco who coined the term "Mochica"—that is, Moche—to replace "Proto-Chimú." He also developed a five-phase ceramic chronology, based on stylistic changes in vessels over time, upon which archaeologists relied for more than half a century.[17] Larco not only published his field investigations but also produced broader interpretations of Moche culture. He built and funded a large museum to display his collection of artifacts from Moche and other ancient cultures.[18]

Other archaeologists and scholars, both Peruvian and foreign, worked on the north coast, but their numbers were few through the 1930s. The situation changed dramatically in 1940 when a team of U.S. archaeologists, encouraged and supported by Larco, launched the Virú Valley Project under the direction of William Duncan Strong of Columbia University, with the collaboration of William Bennett of Yale. Gordon R. Willey, then a graduate student at Columbia, conducted a settlement pattern study that remains a landmark of archaeological investigation. Rather than looking solely at Moche culture, the researchers attempted to document long-term changes in the habitation of the entire valley. Nevertheless, they discovered the so-called Tomb of the Moche Warrior-Priest, the most elaborate high-status Moche burial found until that time. The Virú Valley Project was one of the largest archaeological programs ever conducted in Peru, and its location on the north coast drew attention to the region and the potential for studying its ancient cultures.[19]

After World War II, a number of significant field investigations took place on the north coast. In the late 1960s, Donald Proulx and Christopher Donnan, then graduate students under the direction of John H. Rowe at Berkeley, conducted surveys of valleys at the suspected southern limits of Moche culture, in the Nepeña Valley and the Santa Valley, respectively. In the following years, several projects moved forward under the auspices of the Chan Chan–Moche Valley Project, directed by Harvard's Michael E. Moseley. Teresa L. Topic, who worked at the Huacas de Moche, interpreted Huaca del Sol as an administrative center and Huaca de la Luna as a religious center. Garth Bawden excavated at Galindo and developed a model of the collapse of the Moche regime. Part of the research included excavations of burials in the plain between the Huacas Sol and Luna. Many other scholars who made careers in Andean archaeology also participated in the Harvard project, including Geoffrey Conrad, Richard Keatinge, Alan Kolata, John Topic, and Thomas and Sheila Pozorski.[20]

The great amount of work accomplished by the Harvard project seemed to have provided keys to understanding Moche culture. The Harvard researchers' ideas elaborated on Larco's view of Moche as a single political and cultural entity. But despite an increased interest in things Moche among archaeologists, few members of the Chan Chan–Moche Valley Project continued to work on the topic. One exception was Kent Day, who developed a subsequent project through the Royal Ontario Museum that focused on the site of Pampa Grande. It served as an umbrella for relatively separate projects, including a long-term involvement in the area by Izumi Shimada.

Although no other large field projects took place for many years, Moche studies advanced significantly through smaller excavations and, especially, research on iconography. Christopher Donnan, though also active in field research, devoted a great deal of time and energy to developing the Moche Archive at the University of California, Los Angeles, a collection of many photographs and drawings of painted and molded pottery and other art. Donnan, Gerdt Kutscher, Elizabeth Benson, Anne Marie Hocquenghem, Yuri Berezkin, Jürgen Golte, and other scholars interpreted Moche beliefs and behavior by studying such depictions. This partial list of students of Moche art, including scholars from the United States, Germany, and Russia, among other countries, reflects great international interest in the subject.[21]

An important turning point in Moche archaeology came when Peruvian police halted the looting of the royal tombs at the Moche site of Sipán in 1987 and with subsequent professional excavations there by Peruvian archaeologist Walter Alva.[22] At Sipán, Alva carefully investigated the richest and most complete high-status tombs ever excavated in South America. Despite the looting, Alva's team found three burials of Moche lords, complete with sacrifices of llamas and humans and loaded with necklaces, ear ornaments, and other jewelry and paraphernalia wrought in gold and semiprecious stones. Before that time, huacas had been off limits to archaeological excavation for several reasons. Many archaeologists believed that finding ancient Peruvian gold brought trouble—potential danger to life and limb from robbers and

Gordon R. Willey in the Virú Valley Project. At the time, Willey was a graduate student at Columbia University. Although his career eventually focused on the Maya, especially during his long tenure at Harvard University, his settlement pattern study in Virú was a benchmark in New World archaeology that is still frequently cited. 2002.26.19

possible accusations by colleagues of theft by holding back some of the treasures. Others believed that excavating elaborate tombs was "unscientific," or at least that the great labor necessary to dig them and the attention that doing so might bring would steal time that could be devoted to quieter but more productive pursuits. Some archaeologists even surmised that all the gold had already been looted, a theory that seems not so farfetched when one views the moonlike landscapes of sites that have been looted for centuries. Sipán was a wake-up call that unless archaeologists began to excavate huacas, looters would continue to reap rich harvests, leaving archaeologists and the Peruvian nation deprived of important information and great works of art.

By the early 1990s a new era in Moche archaeology had begun, and it continues today. An important change has been the development of large, ongoing research projects directed by Peruvian archaeologists. Three such projects in particular have been and remain significant. Santiago Uceda and Ricardo Morales, of the National University of Trujillo, have been excavating at the Huacas de Moche in the Moche Valley, particularly at Huaca de la Luna. In the Chicama Valley, a team led by Régulo Franco, César Gálvez, and Segundo Vásquez, with support from the Wiese Foundation in Lima, has worked at the El Brujo archaeological complex, especially at the site of Huaca Cao Viejo. Farther north, long-term research by Luis Jaime Castillo has focused on and around the site of San José de Moro in the Jequetepeque Valley. Significant research has also been carried out by Peter Kaulicke, Kristof Makowski, and others based in Peru, and a host of foreigners—such as Steve Bourget, Claude Chapdelaine, Tom Dillehay, Christopher Donnan, and Jean François Millaire—has contributed much to expanding and deepening our view of the Moche, both in the field and through studies of art.[23]

All that we know about the Moche has grown from the scholarly efforts of the researchers I have mentioned and many more. As the work advanced over the years, the conclusions of one set of scholars became established and served as building blocks for later researchers. Over time, new perspectives raised questions about ideas previously considered to be "facts," and new interpretations were offered. Before I delve into some of these interpretations, I want to review the nature of Moche media, particularly ceramics. I then look at the means by which they and the messages they carried are generally studied and at some issues that arise from such approaches. From there it is possible to probe further into the messages themselves and the people who sent and received them.

Moche portrait head vessel in the form of a bowl. Such vessels more commonly take
the stirrup-spout form. The visage on this pot seems typically calm and contemplative.
The person wears head cloths tied at the back and under the chin. PM 968-14-30/8570
(W 17.3 × H 16 cm). 98540008. Mark Craig, photographer.

Media for Moche Messages

MOCHE PEOPLE, JUST LIKE PEOPLE TODAY, conveyed messages about themselves and their culture through their material objects—pottery, metalwork, textiles, even the enormous huacas as self-consciously designed architecture. Of all these media, researchers have so far studied Moche pottery most closely. They have grouped the entire pottery inventory into three main functional categories: utilitarian wares, serving vessels, and fancy ceramics, known as fine wares (pl. 16). Utilitarian pottery—cooking and storage vessels, for example—was the most simply made, through the use of coils or slabs of clay, and the most crudely formed of the three. Although studies of utilitarian wares could reveal interesting things about the Moche economy and other facets of life, few such studies have been carried out. Utilitarian vessels appear to have been made in ways and put to uses that went relatively unchanged for many years across great areas, so they may not be sensitive markers of contemporary differences or culture change.

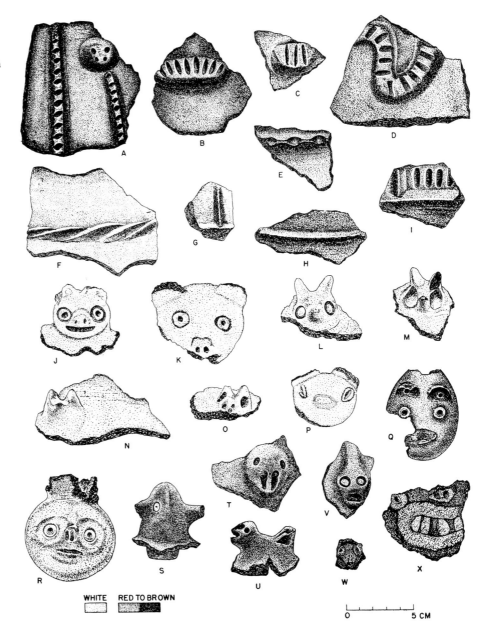

WHITE   RED TO BROWN

0   5 CM

Moche artisans made pottery to be used for eating and drinking with greater care than vessels that were to be subjected to the rigors of cooking fires or storage. Still, they generally gave less attention to the manufacture of serving vessels than they did to the finest Moche ceramics. Besides using jars and bowls for serving food, Moche people used shallow bowls and even ceramic spoons for consuming meals. Among the food-service wares is a distinctive group known as the Castillo series, which includes vessels characterized by quickly made faces with "coffee-bean" eyes and other features. Like utilitarian wares, these vessels were hand built, but they received a few extra treatments such as the eyes and facial features. Apparently the makers added these for amusement rather than to convey profound messages about the cosmos. As in the case of utilitarian wares, few extensive studies of serving vessels have been carried out, even though much could probably be learned from them.

Moche fine wares consist of elaborately made vessels such as those in the Peabody Museum collection and illustrated in most of the plates in this book. Some of these vessels may have played roles in rituals, but many likely had no function other than to convey messages about the owner's prestige during his or her life and to serve as burial offerings in death.[24] Moche fancy ceramics have received the greatest attention from archaeologists and art historians, both because of their appeal to contemporary tastes and because they are thought to be more heavily loaded with information about Moche society, beliefs, cultural differences, and cultural change.

To create Moche fine wares, artisans pressed soft, pliable clay into two or more ceramic molds to create separate parts of the final vessel. Then they "glued" the pieces together using clay slurry. The surface of the vessel was finished by hand polishing, hand painting, or both. Sometimes shell or stone inlays enhanced the final product.

The use of molds permitted Moche craftspeople to create multiples of the same vessel. Archaeologists used to think that using molds might have improved the efficiency of pottery production, allowing for its spread throughout the Moche population. Recent studies suggest that molds did not necessarily improve the speed with which pottery was produced,[25] although they did provide a form of efficiency by freeing potters from having to start from the beginning with every new vessel. They also

A mold used for producing Moche fine-ware figurines. The appearance of a "positive" image in this photograph is an optical illusion. PM 46-77-30/5199 (W 16.5 x H 22.5 cm). 98540023. Mark Craig, photographer.

would have made it possible for workshops to include master artisans who made the molds and less skilled workers who assembled the pieces, which might have aided efficiency. But making molds requires time and effort itself, and molds surely broke eventually and had to be replaced.

Perhaps, then, Moche artisans developed molds not to make ceramic production faster or more efficient but in order to produce duplicates. This proposition rests on a widespread concern with dualism in Andean belief systems. In Andean thought, the entire universe is powered by the dynamism created by two opposite but slightly unequal forces or entities—forces of "asymmetrical dualism"—somewhat similar to the Asian concept of yin and yang. This worldview appears to have great antiquity in Peru and was shared by the people who adopted the Moche religion and art style. In pottery, we may see its manifestation in almost identical pairs of ceramics, which users seem to have desired in certain types of vessels (pl. 22). A mold would have facilitated the creation of such a pair.

The idea of asymmetrical dualism is best known from Inca examples such as the use of pairs of slightly different vessels. Pairs of near equals included males and females, the sun and the moon, and uphill and downhill. In their political and social relations, the Inca expressed the concept of near equality by drinking *chicha,* an alcoholic maize beverage, from vessels of slightly different sizes and decoration; the higher-ranking person used the larger vessel. That we find pairs of Moche drinking vessels in slightly different sizes suggests similar principles and actions among those people as well. Slight differences designed to emphasize the near equality of two vessels could have been achieved by varying the finish or decoration of mold-made pairs of vessels. Dualism is also seen in a host of other objects of Moche material culture, such as pairs of huacas, and in the use of gold and silver ornaments as pairs of the same artifact or sometimes combined in a single object as equal or near-equal metals.

A type of ceramic that archaeologists call "stirrup-spout" vessels (see illustration on p. 48), which the Moche counted among their most favored forms and of which many examples appear in the Peabody collection, probably held great symbolic power. Partaking of the ideology of dualism, these vessels likely signified the important concept of "two things that come together to make one." In Quechua, the Inca language, the place where two different things join is called a *tinkuy*. Such a place is powerful and sacred, whether it is the seam sewn to join two cloths or the confluence of two streams to make a river. The stirrup spout, creating two separate flows of liquid from a common source and then reuniting them in a single spout, expressed tinkuy or a closely related concept.[26]

Yet even as artisans used molds to create closely matched pairs of vessels, they could also recombine the sections produced by molds to make different objects. Varying the painted designs and other decorative techniques applied to vessels also increased the diversity of pots over time.[27] Many vessels seem to have been made from the same or similar molds but with different finishes. The basic portrait head vessel, for example—a characteristic variety of Moche fine ware—could be produced with a large hole at the top, forming a bowl, or, more typically, with the head closed off and topped by a stirrup spout (pls. 11, 12). Given the great length of time during which the Moche style was popular, it is likely that molds served both to diversify a potter's inventory and to make near duplicates at various times and places.

Pottery, with its pervasive symbolism, was a principal medium by which Moche religion was disseminated, but the vessels were not simply conveyers of ideology. They also had value as desired possessions. The fanciest Moche ceramics might have been valued more highly as things unto themselves than for their practical uses. They probably served as status items as well as reminders of religious ideas, much the way decorative plates hung on kitchen walls today serve more to convey values and beliefs than as containers. The Moche even represented vessels, including stirrup-spout pots, *on* their vessels (pl. 8), from which we may infer that the pots themselves were valued.

The discovery of fine wares in the tombs of what appear to be lower-ranking commoners has corrected the assumption that fancy pottery was a prerogative of the Moche elites. Fine vessels apparently were made in quantities great enough that many people beyond the highest-ranking Moche could own them. Of course in making this statement I am applying modern standards of what constitutes a relatively "fine" vessel.[28]

Nor did the elites necessarily receive burial with the finest of wares. In the most elaborate Moche burial excavated to date, the tomb of the Señor de Sipán—the "Lord of Sipán"—archaeologists found 1,137 pottery vessels. Most of them were simple necked jars and vessels in the form of seated or standing men. Traces of any contents that might remain in them have not yet been studied, but it is interesting that few of these vessels would today be considered among the finest examples of Moche ceramic craftsmanship. They were quickly made and poorly painted, with little attention given to detail. According to the excavators, some of the figural vessels were arranged in tableaux, such as a group of pots depicting musicians and prisoners surrounding and facing apparently higher-ranking persons. Other anthropomorphic vessels were arranged marching double file, and still others were placed next to clusters of llama bones or seashells. The overall impression is that the contents of the vessels were less important than the presence of the jars as a symbolic royal retinue or a record of the Señor de Sipán's deeds.[29] Although ceramics, other than this complex arrangement, apparently were not particularly noteworthy in the Sipán tombs, the tombs were extremely wealthy overall, especially in the gold ornaments interred with the dead and the inclusion of sacrificed retainers and llamas in the burials.

Only a few vessels that we would consider "fine" were found at Sipán. One was a ceramic bottle with a "mushroom cap" hat and real metal ear ornaments. In a high niche in the walls of the tomb, near the head of the main burial, pairs of fine-quality stirrup-spout vessels were arranged symmetrically around a centrally placed

Spondylus shell. This find helps to corroborate the view that the ancient Moche shared our contemporary valuation of "fine" vessels; clearly, these examples were important enough to be placed prominently in the tomb of a high-ranking lord.[30] Nevertheless, many fine vessels have been found in lower-status tombs as well—the tombs of what we might consider "middle-class" Moche. The issue of who had access to which kinds of ceramics is still not fully resolved.

Besides pottery, Moche media included many other forms and materials. The large huacas were brightly painted, especially on their front terraces, to impress the great

Artist's conception of what Huaca de la Luna might have looked like at its height. Huaca Cao Viejo was built or remodeled on the same plan. The brightly colored murals at these sites provide perspectives on Moche art and the role of huacas that could not have been gained through ceramics alone. Rendering by Jorge Solorzano courtesy Huaca de la Luna Archaeological Project.

numbers of people gathered in the main plazas below. Interior courts where rituals took place received colorful coats of paint as well. Moche artisans produced textiles, too, although relatively few have so far been recovered. Carvers fashioned wood, stone, and gourds into a variety of objects. One of the most spectacular art forms was metalwork, especially in the form of gold and silver ornaments worn by high-ranking priests, lords, and warriors. Dancing, singing, music, and other performing arts undoubtedly were essential elements in temple and court rituals. They are difficult to identify archaeologically, but we are fortunate to have some remarkable representations of them, such as the ceramic trumpet shown in plate 25.

Putting together the archaeological evidence, we can infer that a visit to a Moche temple would have been an impressive experience in the life of a simple farmer. Such a visit combined elements that we think of as separate parts of life today: religion, entertainment, sporting event, and tourism. Lubricated with plenty of chicha, possibly augmented by a brew made from the hallucinogenic San Pedro cactus, the visitor to a Moche temple would have been confronted with a swirl of color in contrast to the greens and browns of agricultural fields and desert. The thrill of watching brave warriors run naked prisoners through the plaza would have brought cheers and hisses from spectators, their senses heightened and intensified not only by chicha and drugs but also by the bright colors of murals, clothing, and jewelry, the pounding of drums, and the blare of trumpets. Then, at the edge of the uppermost temple terrace, flashes of light from the golden costumes of the priestly god-impersonators would have caught the eyes of the crowd below, as the final acts of the sacrificial rites unfolded. Whether the scene on high was carried out by priests or the gods themselves, the crowd's perception became blurred or irrelevant at the culmination of the rituals.[31] It was these warriors, lords, priests, and gods that were the subject matter of the messages of Moche art.

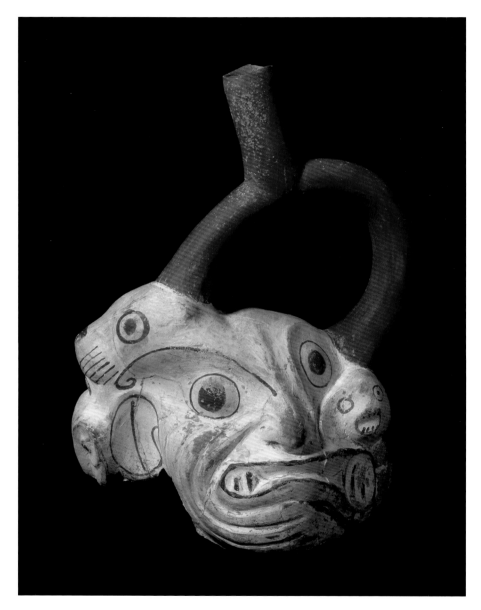

Stirrup-spout vessel in the form of a grotesque face with the heads of an owl, sea
lion, and other creatures emerging from it. Its message is enigmatic, but a key
feature of Andean thought is the mutability of one being or thing into another.
PM 46-77-30/4964 (W 12.5 × H 23.5 cm). 98540059. Mark Craig, photographer.

The Messages of Moche Art

MODELED MOCHE CERAMICS depicting animals as diverse as mollusks, fish, and monkeys, not to mention humans ranging from blind musicians to regal lords, have attracted the attention of museumgoers for more than a century. Most people can look at a Moche vessel and recognize something in it even if they do not understand the symbolic message that the artist intended. Many images, especially modeled figures, seem easily recognizable—a deer, a llama, a person. This representational, or "veristic," style is sometimes said to be unique in the Andes.[32] But if modern political boundaries are ignored, then Moche art is seen to have much more in common with styles to its north than to its south, for the peoples of ancient Ecuador had a long tradition of representational art in clay.

Alfred Kroeber, one of the most prominent anthropologists of the mid-twentieth century, characterized Moche art as "secular."[33] In this he followed an interpretation long voiced in both popular and academic discussions of Moche art, an interpretation that many Moche painted or modeled scenes represented everyday life—for example, a llama with a pack on its back, carrying goods from one place to another, or a war-rior's headdress or helmet (pl. 13). This understanding implied that Moche artisans made these ceramics for secular purposes, such as simply representing their world to themselves.

In the early 1970s, archaeologist Christopher Donnan convincingly demonstrated that what appeared to be depictions of ordinary people and animals were actually highly charged symbols. A deer, for example, was not simply an animal to be hunted but was connected to concepts of prisoners of war and sacrifice, as it was among the Maya. Depictions of deer tied up like prisoners confirmed the connection between the animal and its symbolic role as an analogue or substitute for a human sacrificial victim. Modern scholars have to make such connections through research because they do not participate in the same symbolic system as the Moche. To at least some Moche people, in contrast, a deer depicted by itself might easily have been under-stood as referring to sacrifice, warfare, and elite ritual.

Once scholars began to view Moche art as highly charged with symbolism, new insights into Moche culture and religion accumulated rapidly. A depiction of a woman with a shawl over her head, which might once have been understood simply as a portrayal of a woman, might now, on a number of lines of evidence, be identified as a shaman-curer, or *curandera* (see photographs on pp. 54 (left) and 75, and plate 20). Donnan and his colleague Douglas Sharon used both archaeological data and ethnographic information about contemporary religious practices on the north coast of Peru to investigate such issues.[34] Although Rafael Larco Hoyle and others had earlier followed similar research paths, studies by Donnan, Sharon, and other scholars in the 1970s opened up a new era of in-depth study of the Moche.

Donnan not only recognized that much of Moche art was symbolic but also deter-mined that many painted and modeled representations of gods and other characters interacting were scenes from mythology. Tableaux that he could identify as having specific characters engaged in distinctive ways he referred to as "themes." Some scholars have attempted to reconstruct Moche mythology and ritual behavior by iden-tifying sequential themes.[35] This is no easy task; it resembles trying to construct the

sequence of an unknown movie from snippets of film left on an editing room floor. But with patience and some luck, such efforts can yield interesting results.

Another way to investigate Moche art is to use early colonial period written records that discuss practices and beliefs of native peoples. For example, a myth was told to a Spanish missionary in the central highlands of Peru in the early seventeenth century: In an earlier world era, humanlike inhabitants behaved badly and displeased the gods. As a result, the world was turned upside-down. The sun died, and it was night for five days. Mortars and grinding stones began to eat people, and buck llamas began to drive men instead of being driven by them.

Two well-known Moche pottery vessels seem to depict versions of this story in fine-line painting. Details differ between the story as recounted in the seventeenth century and as shown on the Moche pots; the vessels show rebellion by weapons and military regalia, not by household objects as in the narrated story, and by wild animals such as sea lions and birds, not domesticated beasts. Nevertheless, the pots seem to portray the general theme of a world turned upside-down, making it likely that the myth can be traced far back in time.[36] Such ideas of role reversals were parts of broader concepts

Rollout drawing of the "Revolt of the Objects," a fine-line painting on a Moche vessel now in Berlin. The painting appears to correspond to a version of a myth still extant in Peru in the seventeenth century in which angry gods turn the world upside-down. Drawing by Donna McClelland; reproduction courtesy of her estate.

Earthenware goblet in the form of a snarling deity head. Similar vessels are thought to have contained traces of blood, probably from human sacrifices. The flared pedestal base, a key feature of such ritual vessels, is also a low-pitched rattle, perhaps for use in relatively private rituals. PM 46-77-30/5061 (W 10.2 × H 13.5 cm). 98540007. Mark Craig, photographer.

of the animating spirits in things and their ability— related to the concept of asymmetrical dualism—to be transformed from one state to another.

Archaeological excavations and other fieldwork contribute to understanding Moche art, and in turn, the art studies can enlighten archaeology. To give one example, scenes on pottery depict gods in procession and passing chalicelike cups to one another. Excavations of the tombs of high-ranking Moche at Sipán and San José de Moro revealed the elite dead to be dressed in costumes and paraphernalia like those shown in the art. Accompanying the deceased in the tombs were ceramic chalices like those depicted on the vessels. These lines of evidence, together with the discovery of remains of sacrificial victims at temple sites, led researchers to conclude that the scenes painted on vessels represented the actions not only of gods but also of Moche priests and priestesses. Dressed as gods, they enacted rituals that included sacrificing war prisoners and pouring their blood into cups, possibly to consume it ceremonially. Thus, information drawn from Moche art informed the interpretation of archaeology, which in turn expanded the understanding of the art.[37]

The themes of Moche art seem to cover all aspects of the worlds of nature, humans, and the supernatural. Moche gods are fairly easy to recognize. One sports fangs and distinctive double (figure-eight) ear spools (pls. 23, 24). So, too, an owl dressed as a warrior clearly is not an ordinary bird (pl. 6). Humans appear to be depicted at the other end of the spectrum of anthropomorphic beings. The social roles of some of these figures, such as warriors, are easier to identify archaeologically than others, and often the links between artifacts and social roles are difficult to establish.

Scenes of apparent everyday life and common people appear in Moche art, but most of its subject matter is divinities and elites—rulers, warriors, and priests—and

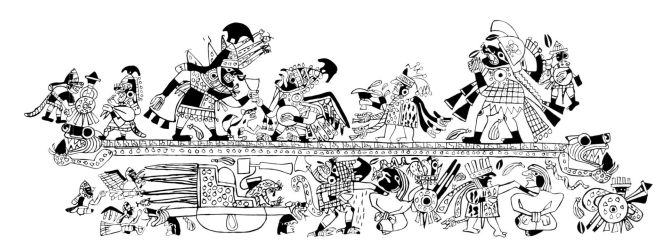

their activities. Although very fine ceramics have been found in burials of people of relatively low rank, the scenes shown on pottery vessels mostly reference rulers and their gods, not the ruled and their folk traditions. Such a pattern is almost universal in ancient complex societies.

Two kinds of Moche pots are particularly well known by the general public: erotic vessels and portrait heads. Although many ancient peoples in both the New and Old Worlds fashioned sculptures that appear erotic or even pornographic to modern eyes, the Moche are famous for the variety of sexual themes they produced. The imagery includes men and women sporting enormous sex organs and couples—animals, humans, or deities—engaged in a variety of sex acts.

It has been noted for some time that most of the activities portrayed on Moche "sex pots" are not those that lead to reproduction. Vaginal intercourse is rarely shown; instead, anal and oral sex acts are portrayed. Steve Bourget believes that such scenes were tied to ideas about the process of moving from life to death and the status of ancestors. He notes that many of the human figures of Moche erotic pottery are skeletons or "skeletonized" humans (pls. 18, 19). From this and other evidence, he argues that erotic pots were references to sex as a source of fertility but also to a world

Rollout drawing of the "Presentation Theme," also known as the Sacrifice Ceremony, in which deities—or human priests dressed as deities—present goblets to a Rayed Deity. At Moche sites, high-status people were sometimes buried wearing costumes portraying some of these deities. Drawing by Donna McClelland; reproduction courtesy of her estate.

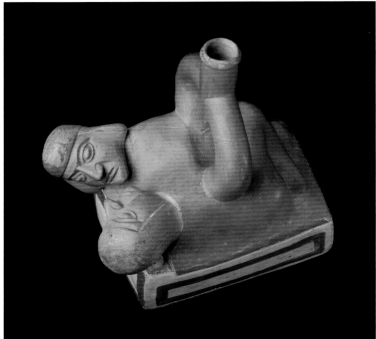

Ceramic vessel portraying a Moche woman, signaled by her long braids and dress. The shawl draped over her head denotes her special shamanic role. PM 968-14-30/8607 (W 13.5 x H 22.5 cm). 98540016. Mark Craig, photographer.

A relatively demure Moche erotic vessel showing a man and a woman covered by a blanket. PM 58-51-30/8165 (W 12.2 x H 17 cm). 98540017. Mark Craig, photographer.

of the dead in which causes and effects were inverted from the land of the living. In other words, whereas reproductive sex occurs in the land of the living, nonreproductive sex is associated with the realm of the dead. Whether all depictions of sex over the entire span of Moche art and throughout the north coast were associated with that specific religious concept must be investigated through further research.[38]

It might be worth considering that although in most societies sexual coupling is thought to have some relationship to procreation, vaginal intercourse does not always result in the birth of a baby nine months after the act. For the Moche, perhaps sex in any form, as a union of two different things, was seen as a particularly powerful and social form of tinkuy, although nonreproductive sex was clearly what they were interested in depicting.

It is also worth considering that at least some sex pots might have been made as a form of humor, as art historian Susan Bergh has discussed.[39] For example, one class of vessels consists of a standing or seated male figure with a huge erection. Although the top of the man's headdress or hat is open, allowing liquid to be poured in, holes around the rim of the headdress cause the liquid to spill on anyone who tries to drink from the hat. The only way to successfully drink from the vessel is via the hole at the end of the over-size penis.

Because humor varies so much in different times and places, archaeologists tend to be wary of attempting to identify examples of it in the past—although many scholars seem to have no trouble identifying some puzzling things as "ritual," which could be argued to be just as problematic as humor. Sex, however, seems to play an almost universal role in humor, so it seems just as plausible that some Moche erotic vessels were used in fun as that they were used in "serious" rituals. The case may never be proved either way —and of course it is possible that a ritual included humor-ous elements. Even so, the existence of more than one possible interpretation of such vessels, and a shortage of evidence to independently support one view over the other, should caution us against making sweeping statements about the nature of Moche art.

Another type of Moche ceramic, the portrait head vessel, stands among the most renowned examples of pre-Columbian art and is the most emblematic example of the Moche "representational" style (pls. 11, 12). The features of individual faces on some of these vessels are so distinctive that they seem to have been modeled on living humans, which gives the category its name. Rafael Larco believed that some of them represented rulers. Such vessels commonly bear stirrup spouts, although many have open tops (see illustration on p. 38). When used, the stirrup spout seems to have been viewed not as modifying the portrait but as an essential aspect of what the

A Moche sense of humor? The opening in the ceramic figure's headdress can be poured into but not drunk or poured from without spilling, forcing the user to consume or pour the liquid from the only available orifice. The skeleton figure may seem frightening, but consider contemporary Halloween imagery as a possible analogue (H 28.6 cm.) ML# 004199. Courtesy Museo Larco, Lima.

vessel was intended to be. The finest examples of portrait vessels do appear to have been modeled on real humans and are arguably among the finest examples of human portraits in the ancient Americas. All of them depict males, of varying ages from young to old, who may wear simple or elaborate headdresses.

Christopher Donnan has identified individuals represented in Moche portrait vessels who appear to have distinctive features, such as a long nose or a scar above the lip. Donnan believes these may have been real, historical persons, and he has nicknamed them according to their distinctive traits: Long Nose, Cut Lip, Black Stripe, and Bigote ("mustache"), among others.

Remarkably, some of these persons are portrayed in stages throughout their lives, from youth to adulthood. In some depictions of Cut Lip in early adulthood, his scar takes a distinctive wishbone shape, but the shape changes in portraits of him as he ages. The example of Cut Lip in the Peabody collection (pl. 11) displays such a wish-bone–shaped scar.

For many of the characters, what is apparently their last portrayal is as a bound sacrificial victim. The depiction of life stages and eventual sacrifice might have been a part of sacrifice rituals, because broken portrait vessels have been found among the remains of adult males slaughtered in a ritual precinct at Huaca de la Luna. Donnan suggests that the most realistic portraits were possibly made in one place and distributed to others. People who received the vessels probably had some special connection to the person portrayed.[40]

How the portrait vessels related to the sacrificial victims is uncertain. One possibility is that at least some portraits represent quasi-historical or mythological figures who were heroes (or villains?), the way Hercules, Achilles, Hector, and Alexander the Great were depicted in Old World Classical antiquity. Why some portrait vessels show the subject at different ages and often in sacrificial victimhood is difficult to explain. Many speculations could be offered, but it does seem that personages from past ages, whether real individuals, mythologized heroes, or completely fictional characters, are the most likely candidates for portrayal at different life stages. Showing them as sacrificial victims could be linked to ideas about brave heroes meeting their deaths for the well being of others, similar to concepts associated with the crucifixion of Christ.

Wooden statuette found as an offering next to the Señora de Cao (height approximately 28 cm). When the nose ornament is removed, a distinctive cut is visible on the figure's upper left lip (detail). The cut is in the same place as that of the "Cut Lip" character identified by Christopher Donnan in portrait head vessels. Photos by the author with permission from Fundación Wiese.

Alternatively, such portrayals might celebrate the end of a mythical or historical character who was brought to justice, as in depictions of the downfall of the devil in some Christian renderings of the triumph of Christ at the Last Judgment. Such characters are also likely to be known by some distinctive trait—the nose, the facial scar—that helps make them easily recognizable, whether by members of the same cultural tradition or some future scholar.[41]

At Huaca Cao Viejo, in the Chicama Valley, a small, carefully made wooden statue of a warrior was discovered buried as an offering in front of an entryway. The statue had no clear portrait features, but a cut was present on the proper left side of its face, immediately above the lip. This figure may be Cut Lip, stripped in this statue of all personality and portraiture and reduced to the iconic, hallmark identification of his distinctive scar. This suggests that some "portraits," although distinctive, might nevertheless have been representations of stock characters from history or myth.

Friezes depicting heads of deities bordered by geometric designs at Huaca de la Luna. Two successive building phases are shown here. The lower patio was used and then filled in with adobe bricks, after which artists created a new frieze on the later upper walls. Although details changed, the general art program was followed repeatedly at the site. Photo by the author.

GODS, PRIESTS, LORDS, WARRIORS, AND HEROES

THE ABUNDANCE OF IMAGES in Moche art makes it difficult to find patterns that can be interpreted as meaningful. Aside from the sources already mentioned, few external references are available to help us interpret the art. Although similar issues of interpretation exist in other fields, we can still look at many examples of European medieval or Renaissance art and know who is being depicted because we have written texts such as the Bible and *Lives of the Saints.* We recognize certain symbols that identify the figures in most European paintings and sculptures, such as Saint Peter's keys, Saint Barbara's tower, and the arrows that pierce Saint Sebastian. Moche gods and heroes almost certainly had such distinguishing features as well, but we cannot always be sure what they are because we lack clear references and often have difficulty distinguishing styles from different times and places. Although sometimes we can recognize characters with specific features, costumes, or paraphernalia, often we can make no finer distinctions or associations, and rarely do we have external evidence to help identify important features in the art. The problem of interpreting Donnan's personages such as Cut Lip is an example of this conundrum.

In order to grapple with these issues, it is important to restate two of the problems confronting researchers who study Moche art and archaeology and to review some case studies. First, many of the ceramic vessels available for study lack precise information about where they were found or where they were originally manufactured and used. Second, although our understanding of changes in Moche ceramic styles over time is undergoing reevaluation, temporal differences still often elude us. Nevertheless, continuing excavations at huacas and other sites are providing new information on Moche art, including murals and friezes as well as metals and other materials found in burials. These new data are helping us to better understand regional and temporal variations in Moche art and their possible significances.

One of the main characters portrayed throughout most of the Moche sequence is an anthropomorphic being with fangs. Rafael Larco dubbed him "Aipaec," using the word for "creator" in the historic north coast language Muchik.[42] Sometimes Aipaec's head is portrayed by itself, but in other scenes he is shown as a complete figure engaged in activities with other characters. His key characteristics appear to be, first, that he is fundamentally anthropomorphic—he resembles a human in his general body and facial features. Because no mortal sports such prominent canines, his fangs tell us that he is a deity, and his double ear spools also seem significant. The figure is commonly shown wearing a belt with loose ends or attachments ending in feline snake heads (see pl. 7). These features are fairly consistent, whereas other details vary. A crucial question is whether these variations represent different aspects of a single deity or different gods.

One Moche god is commonly shown in a frontal position, holding a severed head in one hand and either a crescent-bladed knife or a distinctive chisel-like instrument in the other (pl. 23). The figure appears to be a version of Aipaec, because whether depicted in full figure or as a head only, he sports distinctive double ear spools.[43] The chisel is sometimes shown with an elaborate top, so that it appears to have served also as a scepter. An example of this object was found archaeologically at Sipán. It might have been used to puncture the jugular veins of sacrificial victims in order to draw

Frieze depicting the Degollador God at Huaca Cao Viejo. The two renditions, one with a yellow and the other with a blue background, decorated the front of a corner room facing a large patio during a relatively early building stage of the huaca. Photo by the author.

blood. The deity has been called the Decapitator God when he holds the crescent knife, and with the chisel, he is known as the Degollador, or Throat Cutter—although Peruvianists sometimes use the terms casually and interchangeably.[44]

Still another fanged, anthropomorphic deity is known as "Wrinkle Face." His main characteristics are his wrinkled face, usually depicted in paintings by lines on his cheeks (pls. 21, 22), and a belt with snake heads at the ends. Whereas Aipaec-Decapitator is usually shown standing frontally or simply as a face, Wrinkle Face usually appears in narrative scenes. Often he is accompanied by an anthropomorphic iguana that seems to be a kind of sidekick in a series of adventures, mostly battling monsters such as giant crabs and mollusk–feline creatures.[45]

Many students of Moche iconography distinguish between Aipaec–Decapitator and Wrinkle Face as two or even three separate deities. The matter is complex, though, because some versions of Wrinkle Face show him with double ear spools or the snake–headed belt, features that also identify Aipaec–Decapitator. Such portrayals seem to be more common in relatively early Moche pottery. In other cases, Wrinkle Face sports no wrinkles or only a few and is instead identified primarily by his fangs, his two–headed serpent belt, or the fact that he is accompanied by Iguana.[46]

How many gods are there? It is difficult to know. Because these are gods, it is possible that the differences between them represent changes in Moche religion over time or variations in religion across the Moche region, even if the basic pantheon remained relatively constant, as Donnan has suggested. Changes over time might have included the merging of earlier deities into a single god, the emphasizing of one aspect of a god over others, the promotion of minor deities into major ones, and the retirement of major deities to lesser roles. Similarly, more regional variation might have existed in Moche religion than we can currently account for, or perhaps both regional and temporal variability influenced the depictions. As in so many other issues surrounding the interpretation of Moche culture, the fact that so much of the data comes from looted artifacts only compounds the uncertainty.

One way out of the conundrum of distinguishing between portrayals of Moche gods that share so many attributes is to consider them all part of a Moche "principal god complex." The idea that one deity or the whole Aipaec–Decapitator–Wrinkle Face complex was the principal god can itself be debated, but certainly these faces and figures, which appear so frequently in murals and on pottery, must have been of great concern to the Moche. If the different renditions of the god—standing frontally or staring out from a mural versus taking part in narrative action—are not merely regional or temporal variations, then perhaps they serve different purposes.

Art in which the god is shown in a static position might be called the iconic mode, a form of what anthropologist Sherry Ortner called a "summarizing symbol."[47] A summarizing symbol embodies a great range of beliefs, ideas, and emotions, summing up much if not all of a religion. It collapses and condenses complex ideas and experiences into a single, powerful image. A cross or crucifix does this for Christianity. Aipaec's head and the Decapitator standing with a severed head and knife likely were similar summarizing symbols.

Wrinkle Face, however, is usually shown engaged in some activity, often combat, in what can be called a narrative mode. Ortner refers to such kinds of scenes as "elaborating symbols." They are key scenarios providing cultural orientations to proper behavior or the nature of the world and demonstrating the culturally appropriate means to achieving certain ends. For an analogy, the "means–to–ends" idea can be seen in Horatio Alger's stories of young men working hard to achieve success. The message is, "If you work hard (means), you will succeed (ends)." These stories are examples of secular elaborating symbols in Anglo–American culture. Tales of Superman and other caped crusaders are similar secular symbols, although they skirt the boundaries of religion in that the superheroes fight for high ideals—"Truth, Justice, and the American Way."[48] The narrative scenes of Wrinkle Face and other fragments of stories depicted on Moche art likely served the same kinds of functions. They did not literally tell humans to fight crab monsters but offered a view of "how the world really is" by depicting events from which humans could draw lessons.

Approaching Moche art using Ortner's concepts of summarizing and elaborating symbols may not answer all our questions about the scenes depicted, but it might help us to better understand some apparently odd scenes that appear. For example, a scene known from several instances shows Wrinkle Face apparently dazed, ill, or otherwise incapacitated, supported on either side by two figures (pl. 21). Often, one of Wrinkle Face's eyes appears different from the other, suggesting that he has sustained an injury. By itself this scene appears not to show the god at his best. But if we consider it part of a narrative in which Wrinkle Face goes through some adversity, we can appreciate the scene—part of a larger story into which we have only glimpses—as an elaborating symbol. Indeed, the curing scene depicted on one of the Peabody Museum's bottles (pl. 20) might be part of this longer story.

Taking the iconic and narrative pictorial modes into account, we can consider issues of art and its reception. Both modes can be successfully employed only with an audience already familiar with the ideology that the iconic symbols summarize and the longer stories explain. Otherwise, the images would be incomprehensible or meaningless, as they often are to viewers today. Moche artists or their patrons might have had many reasons for wanting to tell stories, and they employed both the narrative and the iconic modes from early times. Christopher Donnan and Donna McClelland noted that paintings on early Moche pots (Phases I and II in the chronology developed by Rafael Larco) tend to depict supernaturals and their activities.[49] After this, the depiction of apparently human activities increased dramatically. By Phase IV, probably in the late sixth century or the seventh, human and supernatural activities seem to have been equally represented. In Phases IV and V, the trend reversed: nearly all painting, now done in the fine-line style, depicted supernaturals as parts of narratives.[50] A shift is also seen at this time in that "new" gods, or possibly reconfigured, reinterpreted, or "promoted" old gods, such as the Owl Deity, came to the fore.

Another trend over time is that Moche artists increasingly placed more images and therefore more information on their vessels. This development might signal important changes in the relationship between senders and recipients of the messages carried by Moche media. The use of a single image or a few of them suggests that viewers shared an understanding of the represented symbolism. In addition, such images can be identified and understood from fairly far away. An average-size Moche pot or a large modeled or painted image can be interpreted from a distance of 10 feet or more. Such iconic images, then—a form of easily read "shorthand"—might have been viewed by relatively large audiences, reminding them of the tenets of Moche religion.

Narrative scenes, on the other hand, consist of many smaller, painted images that can be comprehended only upon close inspection, by one or two persons looking at the object at a time. The loading of pottery vessels with dense imagery suggests that elaborating symbols were being presented, perhaps conveying new messages that had to be presented in extended narrative form. Because such imagery had to be read at close range, it might have been intended only for the owner of the vessel and his or her close associates.

Our understanding of shifting Moche ceramic styles and changing symbolic content has recently been complicated by the recognition of different, contemporaneous styles in different parts of the north coast. In order to explore this issue thoroughly, I want next to look at some of the issues associated with understandings of Moche political systems. For Moche scholars, ceramic styles have been used to interpret politics, and vice versa.

The burial of a priestess at San José de Moro, Jequetepeque Valley. Large metal arms, legs, mask, and headdress decorations in the burial (now corroded to green) were mounted on the sides of a coffin, which has deteriorated. Photo Courtesy Proyecto San José de Moro, Catholic University of Peru.

Media, Messages, Religion, and Politics

SCHOLARS HAVE MADE GREAT STRIDES in identifying gods and even specific rituals represented in Moche art, but what can the art reveal about the way people on the north coast of Peru organized themselves politically? Archaeologists, including Rafael Larco, originally thought of Moche art as a single, uniform style that developed in a single, uniform chronological sequence and was the expression of a single, unified political state. Larco believed the Moche state had originated in the Moche and Chicama valleys and had a single capital, the Huacas de Moche site complex. Members of Harvard's Chan Chan–Moche Valley Project expanded on this idea in the 1970s, suggesting that rulership at Huacas de Moche was divided between a civil authority, with its headquarters at Huaca del Sol, and a religious hierarchy, presiding at Huaca de la Luna.

As archaeologists began working on the north coast outside the Moche and Chicama valleys, they sometimes observed traits in artifacts that did not conform to what they understood as the Moche style. For example, ceramics of the Vicús archaeological culture, known since the mid-1960s from the area near the modern town of Piura, north of the Moche heartland, looked more Ecuadorian than Moche but still shared some Moche traits. Vicús metalwork looked much like that of Moche but seemed technologically more advanced.

Another anomaly came from the Gallinazo site, in the Virú Valley, immediately south of the Moche Valley.[51] There, one subset of the Gallinazo style was the Castillo series, mentioned previously as mid-quality serving wares. In the Virú Valley, Castillo series ceramics appeared not only at the Gallinazo site but also at many sites otherwise considered to be Moche, alongside fancy Moche ceramics. Fieldwork and examination of collections suggested that Gallinazo culture lasted well into the Moche era. Archaeologists explained the anomaly by suggesting that Moche and Gallinazo people lived side by side in the same settlements, each group practicing its own ceramic traditions, or perhaps the Moche conquered the Gallinazo and absorbed them into their own culture.

In the late 1990s, as field research intensified, Christopher Donnan and Luis Jaime Castillo developed a strong argument, based largely on differences in ceramic styles, that two different Moche regions had existed, one in the north and the other in the south. Separating the two was the Pampa de Paiján, one of the broadest of the coastal deserts, between the Chicama and Jequetepeque valleys. Many scholars currently accept the Donnan and Castillo proposal. Only a few still adhere to the idea of a single, expansive Moche state, although many believe that the southern Moche realm was a single state that grew southward from its capital at the Huacas de Moche. Another school of thought proposes that Moche architectural centers in different valleys were independent of one another. Recently, Donnan, Castillo, and Santiago Uceda have all begun to identify what appear to be substyles of Moche ceramics. Rather than a single Moche political unit that encompassed all the northern valleys, the view is emerging that different "Moches" existed in different valleys.

In the lower Jequetepeque Valley, Castillo traced the development of irrigation canals and concluded that areas watered by different canal systems likely were the most important political units in the valley. Small settlements are scattered across the unirrigated parts of the valley, and many of these habitation zones include small platforms and other indications of local ceremonial architecture. They also feature defensive walls, bastions, and sometimes piles of sling stones—ammunition for the primary long-distance weapon of ancient Peruvian warriors.

The largest ceremonial site in the lower Jequetepeque Valley is San José de Moro. It consists of two medium-size huacas and many layers of burials in the flat areas between and around the mounds. Several high-status women were buried near the base of one huaca, dressed in costumes depicted in Moche art as being worn by a woman deity. San José de Moro was apparently particularly devoted to this goddess, and these women served in succession as her priestesses, either by appointment or by inheritance. Other high-status people buried at the site were accompanied by elaborate and plentiful tomb offerings and occasionally by sacrificial victims. During the use of the cemetery, people used the area to prepare food and chicha. This practice was almost certainly associated with yearly or seasonal pilgrimages by the kin of the deceased to bury, celebrate, and feast their ancestors.

Castillo combines the evidence for the canal systems, the habitation zones with their platforms and defenses, and the burials and other information from San José de Moro to produce a convincing picture of the relations between politics, economics, and religion during middle to late Moche times in the Jequetepeque Valley. Whereas the earlier view of a Moche conquest state saw huaca centers sending armies and art styles outward with a kind of centrifugal force, Castillo's model sees San José de Moro as a centripetal power, pulling people and resources to it. As a religious center, San José de Moro appears to have been a place where high-ranking regional elites wished to be buried. It might also have been a place where they went to parlay with one another to iron out their political differences in a setting that combined features of today's United Nations and the Vatican. The priestesses and other religious officials might have served as mediators or arbiters in such regional disputes.

A long tradition exists in the Andes in which important religious centers served also as oracle centers. Several are known for Inca times, and at least one, at Chavín de Huantar, has been inferred for more remote antiquity. Although variability in social and cultural practices surely was considerable throughout the millennia of Andean civilization and across a vast region, the possibility that the priests and priestesses of

Modern woman dressed as the Señora de Cao. Her clothing and ornaments are replicas of those found in her tomb at Huaca Cao Viejo. Courtesy Fundación Wiese.

On the north coast of Peru, shamans are well known to effect cures of physical, psychological, and spiritual illnesses, now as in the past.[54] Contemporary shamans employ objects and symbols associated with prehistoric cultures, and archaeologists find substantial evidence that healers followed similar practices in prehistory. Indeed, one of the most discussed Moche objects in the Peabody collection is a stirrup-spout bottle depicting a woman-bird shaman apparently in the act of ministering to an ill Wrinkle Face (pl. 20). This is a supernatural curing ceremony, but it almost certainly mimics actual Moche curing sessions.

In the tomb of the Señora de Cao, excavators found a stirrup-spout bottle that also appears to depict a curing session. Modeled in clay, a mother presents her nursing infant daughter to a curandera, who wears a distinctive shawl also seen in other renditions of women engaged in such acts. The curandera touches the baby's abdomen, either as a blessing or as a cure. No definitive evidence demonstrates that fine-ware bottles placed in tombs referred directly to the roles or activities of the deceased, but it seems more than coincidental that a bottle showing a woman performing a cure accompanied this high-ranking woman in death.

Castillo's argument for understanding San José de Moro as a neutral place of negotiation cannot be extended with rigorous "proof" to other huaca centers such as Huaca Cao Viejo, where the Señora de Cao was buried. It does, however, satisfactorily account for many features of the current archaeological data. And because curing was at least partly a spiritual endeavor in ancient Peru, perhaps it is not too great a logical leap to infer that high-ranking women who played such roles were also understood to channel or connect to supernatural realms for other purposes, such as oracular divination. Considering Castillo's interpretation of San José de Moro, it follows that priestesses and, likely, priests served also to mediate between earthly and celestial realms, taking on roles as oracles and curanderos as well as those of god enactors carrying out ritual performances.

Castillo's close analysis of the Jequetepeque Valley reveals a fractured and contentious political landscape. Meanwhile, archaeologists working in other northern Moche valleys are beginning to identify local ceramic styles. The evidence no longer supports the concept of a uniform, "corporate" Moche style associated with a single, expansive Moche state. Instead, many styles drew upon similar ideas and used similar artistic conventions. The degree to which local ceramic styles corresponded to political units will certainly be studied in the future, and it seems likely that similar intensive, long-term studies in the southern Moche area will uncover the same sorts of local phenomena—the "many Moches"—that Castillo and others have discovered in the north. And although I have made a case for huaca complexes as oracular centers, I believe that they served other purposes as well. Huacas might have been different things in different places, and their roles probably changed during the many centuries over which the Moche phenomenon endured.

Nevertheless, some kind of spread of Moche culture does appear to have taken place, likely emanating from the Huacas de Moche and influencing people farther south. It was less a strictly political movement, however, with armies marching to dominate others, than the spread of a religious complex to which economic and political components were intimately tied.

Armies did march throughout the Moche region, but the earliest cadres were likely based not at huaca centers but at the many sites in the region that appear to be cities, such as Mocollope (see the photograph on p. 78). This and other sites do have ceremonial structures in them, but they are much more urban than religious in their organization. This may have changed over time. Although huaca centers might have begun as places of pilgrimage and negotiation, perhaps they eventually became power centers themselves. And taking a more active role in political affairs might ultimately have led to their downfall. Many centers might have vied for attention, but the particular religious system that apparently began at Huaca de la Luna seems to have risen to prominence, influencing populations in other valleys. Eventually, though, the religious cult and prominence of Huaca de la Luna and Huaca del Sol waned, and new systems of social relations and religion became prominent. In the south, in the Moche Valley itself, the new order was signaled at the site of Galindo, whereas in the north the massive complex of Pampa Grande rose to power. These developments came at the end of the Moche era and expressed changes that became more pronounced as Moche faded from the archaeological record, to be succeeded by a murky time of transition out of which emerged the Lambayeque culture in the old northern Moche zone and the Chimú culture in the southern Moche region.

A section of the ruins of Mocollope, a Chicama Valley site that appears to have been a city more than a religious complex. It includes large halls and many smaller buildings. Photo by the author.

Reconsidering Moche

ARCHAEOLOGISTS' UNDERSTANDING of Moche culture has evolved from considering the ceramics and huacas as representing a distinct "people"—*the* Moche—to seeing many Moches. But conceiving of peoples as congruent with sets of traits—crafts, tools, architectural forms, and artistic styles—is an abstraction made by scholars; it is not the way the people themselves thought of their identities as they lived them. Whether we see one Moche or many, the heart of the issue is what the Moche art style and its associated traits mean in terms of human thought and behavior.

Even when Larco's five-phase ceramic sequence was the accepted chronology for the entire Moche region, researchers had trouble identifying the earliest phase, Moche I, and it is still elusive. Moche I ceramics looked much like the earlier Salinar ceramic style, among others. In such cases, archaeologists usually claim that more research is needed to find the missing data. But perhaps the "missing" Moche I will never be found because it did not exist. Instead, a gradual shift in symbolism and styles may have taken place almost imperceptibly. What many see as a generalized Moche art style and religious system grew locally, in different north coast valleys, partly from new ideas, partly from communication among the peoples of the region, and partly from ancient traditions. Santiago Uceda has argued, for example, that the supernaturals depicted on the front terrace murals at Huaca de la Luna are direct descendents of the earlier gods of Chavín.

Although Moche culture may have grown from local roots, current scholarly trends that see many Moches should be counterbalanced by recognizing that these different Moches still express a recognizable unity. Even if the beginning and end of Moche are fuzzy, there is something coherent and identifiable—a "Mocheness"—in the archaeological record. It is most apparent in the ceramics commonly dubbed Phases III and IV, coalescing in its distinctive form sometime between A.D. 450 and 650. Inferentially, at some point and at some place or places, something uniquely "Moche" seems to have held sway. I believe the various local cults and practices that produced similar-looking pottery were reinterpreted and codified in the Chicama and Moche valleys, especially at Huaca Cao Viejo and Huaca de la Luna. The Huacas de Moche became the center and transmitter of distinct religious practices, the "classic" southern Moche culture that has been interpreted in the past as an expansionist state.

In the Moche Valley, people built and rebuilt the huge adobe temple of Huaca de la Luna over many centuries. The rebuilding projects simply encased earlier constructions in new adobes, like the layers of an onion or a set of Russian dolls. Most huacas bear evidence that work crews built sections of walls during each construction phase. Slight variations in the sizes of bricks as well as visible separations between large blocks of stacked adobes attest to this construction technique. In addition, "makers' marks"—an X, a diagonal line, a spiral, or some other simple design—are found on some bricks. They suggest that someone kept a tally of the contributions of different work gangs in building wall sections.

Archaeologists have removed the tumbled-down adobes to reveal earlier layers in deeper excavations. As deep as they have been able to go, the archaeologists have found the same decorative pattern on the interior walls of chambers in the temple.

The Prisoner Frieze at Huaca de la Luna. The frieze covered both the front of the huaca (seen at rear right) and at least one plaza wall (foreground). Photo by the author.

The pattern consists of diamond-shaped bas-reliefs with the face of Aiapec grimacing in the centers (see illustration on p. 58). Despite minor variations in the treatment of this decorative program, the basic motifs began very early in the life of the site and remained constant to its end.

Excavations of the front terraces of Huaca de la Luna have also revealed multiple remodelings featuring the same set of images on seven terraces. These images consist of deities and mythological heroes on the upper terraces, whereas the two lowest terraces seem to portray more human activities: warriors bringing in naked prisoners linked by ropes around their necks while on the terrace above them officials hold hands and dance or sing, as if they are cordoning off the procession of victorious warriors and sacrificial prisoners. Earlier depictions of these themes were painted as murals on flat surfaces, but in the last major remodeling the images were created

in painted adobe bas-relief. Artists took a technique that formerly had been used only for interior patios and applied it to exterior terraces. The terrace bas-reliefs, or friezes, were likely redone a number of times before the site was abandoned.[55]

At Huaca Cao Viejo, in the Chicama Valley, the artistic program for most of its many building phases followed a pattern different from that at Huaca de la Luna. At Huaca Cao Viejo, the terraces were painted in solid colors, alternating in hues of red, white, and yellow at some times and simply in red and white at others. Interior patios were adorned not with repeating images of Aipaec but with maritime themes and stylized representations of freshwater catfish. Artisans decorated the walls of the Señora de Cao's patio, for example, with geometric renderings of sea life. On one side of the patio's small corner room appeared checkerboard arrangements of deities, and on the other, a checkerboard of a dragonlike creature sometimes referred to as the "Moon Animal."

In the last major building phase at Huaca Cao Viejo, artists abandoned the previous decoration programs and instead followed the designs of the bas-reliefs of the

as emblematically "Moche" today. The individuals or kin groups who subscribed to the ideas and practices of the huaca centers entered into a new set of social relations in which temple officials were in charge—or at least that was the priests' aim.

After several centuries of widespread "Mocheness," the system, whatever its on-the-ground form from one place to another, finally fell apart. Whether or not El Niño weather played a role in its demise, one critical fact of life held sway on the north coast of Peru that the temple priests were never fully able to overcome. The underlying contradiction in their attempts to gain control over valley populations was that the production of essentials—mostly farm produce and foods from the sea—remained in the hands of the common people of the valleys and shores. Those people and their labor were almost certainly organized along lines of kinship, as is known for the north coast in later times. What the Moche system may have offered was a "new world order" in which kin relations came secondary to participation in the political entity represented by the huaca centers. Priests and rulers tried to convince lower-ranking members of society that the elites' privileged positions were "natural," perhaps god given. They appear to have been successful at this for a long time, convincing the members of many kin groups, or at least their leaders, that accepting the Moche system was the right thing to do.

But these are terms in which anthropologists think. The Moche themselves almost certainly would have found them foreign. Rather, they lived out their lives and schemed their schemes within conceptions of the world very different from our own. Whether they were priests performing rituals atop brightly painted temples or poor agriculturalists piling adobe brick on top of adobe brick, they made the best of the world they lived in and tried to manipulate the "system," as they saw it, to their own advantage.

The Moche ceramics of the Peabody collection, the many other spectacular Moche artifacts in museums throughout the world, and the huacas that still rise above the agricultural fields on the north coast of Peru are testaments to the complex world in which lived Moche priests, lords, warriors, artisans, fisherfolk, and farmers. In many ways, we are only beginning to appreciate the richness of that past and the lessons it may impart for our own lives.

Photographs of Moche pottery in the collections of the Peabody Museum mounted on a board for use in the classroom. Known as "H-Boards" at Harvard, where they came into use in the 1920s, such aids were widely used throughout academe before projected slides became common. 98700046. PM 2004.29.9592, 2004.29.9593, 2004.29.9594, 2004.29.9595, and 2004.29.9596. Copyright © by the President and Fellows of Harvard College.

The Peabody Museum Collection

THE MOCHE ARTIFACTS HELD by the Peabody Museum at Harvard University consist primarily of ceramic vessels. Many of these were acquired in 1915–1916 through the aid of Julio C. Tello, who was an undergraduate at Harvard at the time. Tello later followed a career in archaeology. He earned an international reputation and today is considered one of the founding fathers of Peruvian archaeology.

Other vessels were collected by Samuel K. Lothrop, a curator at the Peabody Museum for many years, in the early to mid-1940s. Alfred M. Tozzer, a famed Mesoamericanist, and other donors contributed additional pottery, again in the 1940s or earlier. A large group of vessels in the Peabody collection was exported from Peru, with permission, in 1944. About half this group was described as "objects thrown away by *huaqueros* [looters]." Since those times, no artifacts have been acquired except through excavation and with the permission of Peruvian governmental authorities.

The Peabody collection is important for its great number of vessels, its fine examples of Moche art, and the great amount of information the objects convey about Moche culture. The ceramics have delighted and informed Harvard students in classes and the general public in exhibits for many years. They also form one of the important collections used by generations of scholars to interpret Moche culture. Among others, Christopher B. Donnan relied greatly on the collection in his initial studies of Moche art.

No details are known regarding the original locations of these objects when they were last touched by Moche hands. Judging from style, however, all the ceramics illustrated in the following plates, and most of those in the Peabody collection, appear to come from the southern Moche region. Although notes on the artifacts in the Peabody Museum catalogue are brief, they commonly give some information about places of origin. A few state only "north coast"; others note "La Libertad," the Peruvian department that includes the valleys of the Jequetepeque, Chicama, Moche, Virú, and Chao rivers and the north side of the Santa River. The notes for many artifacts state that they are from the Chicama Valley, with lesser representation from the Virú and Moche valleys. Among the ceramics from the Chicama Valley, many also are noted to have come from Sausal, a site near where the narrow middle valley begins to fan out into a broad floodplain. Sausal and some other sites are sometimes referred to with the designation "hacienda," because until relatively recently, large estates were the primary ways in which to refer to locales within the valleys. In the plate captions, valley and more specific designations are supplied when they exist in the records. In their absence, the best available information is provided, usually "La Libertad." The phase designations in the captions refer to Rafael Larco Hoyle's chronology of ceramic styles, Phases I–V.

Color Plates

PLATE 1

Florero with catfish design
46-77-30/4933
Chicama Valley, Hacienda Sausal
Moche, Phase III
Earthenware, red and white paint
Width 22.5 cm, height 13 cm

THE SHAPE OF THIS VESSEL marks it as a *florero* ("flower pot"), a distinctive, diagnostic form of Moche ceramics. Judging from the care taken in shaping and decorating them, floreros are examples of fine ware, but they nevertheless appear to have been functional, serving some unknown purpose. With their wide mouths, the vessels could have held either liquids or solids.

Wide-mouth bowls appear in several Moche scenes modeled or painted on ceramic vessels, but rarely are they shown in enough detail to reveal their contents. One scene of shamanic curing (pl. 20) shows an empty florero in front of a healer. Perhaps such vessels held materials used in healing. Possibly they were even filled with liquid to serve as divinatory mirrors, somewhat like crystal balls, enabling the user to see into the other world and find a cure.

The design on the side of this vessel is a series of heads of a freshwater catfish linked by flowing bands that reflect the "whiskers" of the fish, curving down and then upward from the central head. The white background forms two sets of wave scrolls, one around either side of the back of the head and the other around each whisker. The alternation of the positions of the heads—one facing downward and the next upward—also creates reflected versions of the wave motifs, lending the design on the vessel a subtle but substantial element of dualism.

The fish, called a *life* (pronounced "lee-fay") in Peru, inhabits rivers and irrigation canals, so it is symbolically associated with agriculture rather than with maritime resources. Yet the wave scrolls make the connection among all waters as ultimately linked to the great mother sea, known to the Incas as Mamacocha. The *life* is seen frequently in the art of Huaca Cao Viejo, in the Chicama Valley. This vessel came from the same valley, although from a site farther inland. (98540002. Mark Craig, photographer.)

PLATE 2

Stirrup-spout bottle depicting
a Muscovy duck
09-3-30/75626.6
Department of La Libertad
Moche, Phase IV
Earthenware, red, white, and
orange paints
Width 12 cm, height 28 cm

THE BIRD ON THIS VESSEL is a Muscovy duck (*Cairina moschata*), judging by its feather crest and the fleshy growth, known as a caruncle, over the base of its upper bill. Although it is commonly said to have been domesticated, the species is famous for its belligerence, and the bird is not easily controlled or confronted. It lives in swamps, lakes, and streams and sometimes roosts in trees at night. Aggressiveness is expressed mostly by males, who fight over food, territory, and mates. These qualities drew the attention of the Moche and served as symbolic references for warriors and lords. The Lord of Sipán was buried with elaborate ear spools decorated with Muscovy ducks, likely an expression of his status as a fierce warrior.

The flowerlike designs and paintings of insects on the stirrup spout of this vessel may have carried symbolic meanings that are now difficult to understand. Plants and small animals, including insects, make up the diet of the Muscovy duck. The tall, thin stirrup spout is typical of late Moche ceramics.[57] The orange color is rare. Such tricolor vessels might have been related to a particular site or perhaps were products of a single ceramic workshop. (Opposite: 98540020; far left: 98540063; left: 98540064. Mark Craig, photographer.)

THE STIRRUP SPOUT of this vessel has broken off. The figure that remains is a recumbent camelid with a rolled bundle on its back. The four forms of Andean camelids recognized by the inhabitants of South America are the llama, the alpaca, the guanaco, and the vicuña. These are often classed as separate species, although the issue is debated. Andean people domesticated the first two, including crossbreeds of them; the latter two are wild.

Llama pack trains greatly aided ancient Peruvians in transporting goods from one place to another. Llamas are highland creatures, and for many years researchers debated whether they appeared on the coast only during trading missions, when they descended briefly from the sierra, or whether people kept herds permanently on the coast, outside of their natural range. Further study has confirmed that coastal populations of camelids existed. These included animals with short, strong legs, specially bred to serve as pack animals, and a particular coastal crossbreed between a llama and an alpaca known as a *warizo*. The portrayal in this vessel emphasizes the creature's eyelashes, and indeed, long lashes stand out as an attractive feature to breeders of camelids today.

The elaborately decorated bundle suggests that this animal is carrying something special, but we do not know what the bundle contains or why the llama is shown kneeling. Other examples show rather plain bundles, whereas this one is a decorated textile, perhaps a sign of contents of high value.

A likely possibility is that this is a burial bundle containing the body of a person of high status. The themes of many Moche ceramics have to do with burial, the after-life, and deities. High-status Moche were sometimes buried in wooden or cane coffins, but some were wrapped in bundles (see pl. 19). Missing or misplaced bones in excavated burials indicate that some Moche were buried after the body had begun to decompose. The remains might have been kept in a huaca, or temple, before interment, and burials were sometimes relocated from one tomb to another within a huaca. The relatively small scale of this llama's bundle might indicate that the body is small, possibly that of a young person, although issues of scale may have been of little concern to the vessel's maker. (Opposite: 98540044; inset: 98540045. Mark Craig, photographer.)

PLATE 4

Jar depicting a fanged head
09-3-30/75630
Chicama Valley
Moche, Phase IV
Earthenware, red and white paints
Width 10.4 cm, height 12 cm

THE FANGED HEAD OF THIS VESSEL surmounts three tapering, tuberlike objects that appear to be plants. Because they are so stylized, their identification is uncertain, but they may be a cluster of sweet potatoes (*Ipomoea batatas*) or, more likely, manioc (*Manihot esculenta*) roots. The white designs painted on the back of the figure's head may be manioc "eyes," similar to those on potatoes. Whatever the vegetable is, the

fanged head suggests that plants were spiritually animated, containing an inherent life force. The deity appears to be the one known as "Wrinkle Face," although here he is clearly transformed into a plant or a plant manifesting a quality of the deity. Either this is a general reference to the life force in plants or it refers to a specific story about an animated plant or a deity as a plant. A precise interpretation is elusive, as is the intended use of this vessel and the few other known examples like it.

With its open mouth, the vessel could have been filled with liquid more easily than could a stirrup-spout bottle. Because it depicts a god or hero, we may infer that it was not made for everyday use. The jar likely saw use either for offerings, such as those that might be made at a funeral, or for the consumption of beverages in some ceremonial setting. The most likely beverage would have been chicha, fermented maize, or perhaps manioc. Although we might assume that the combination of plant and deity in this jar implies a ceremony involving fertility, it is equally possible that it marked a more complex mythic concept, now lost. (Opposite: 98540043; left: 98540042. Mark Craig, photographer.)

PLATE 5

Stirrup-spout bottle depicting
a hunt scene
46-77-30/4978
Chicama Valley, Hacienda Sausal
Moche, late Phase IV
Earthenware, red and white paints
Width 8.5 cm, height 30.5 cm

THE ARTIST WHO DECORATED this late Moche vessel with fine-line painting used several methods to create a small masterpiece. The dark red bands around the base and equator of the vessel unite with the color of the top circle, the arc of the stirrup, and the vertical line of the spout. A visual rhythm is created by the alternation of deer and stylized nets arranged in a checkerboard pattern above and below the median band.

Deer hunting was the prerogative of high-status Moche. Apparently at least one method of hunting involved using nets to drive deer into an enclosed space and then killing them with darts thrown with spear throwers or with clubs (see p. 16). Deer hunting by means of nets is one of the most ancient themes depicted in Andean art. Recently, archaeologists discovered a mural showing this practice at the site of Ventarrón, in the Lambayeque Valley, dating to about 2000 B.C.

There is much subtlety in this vessel. It shows human action, but only indirectly, offstage. Many darts surround each deer, suggesting a fury of action, but we see only the aftermath. Most of the darts have apparently missed their mark and lie uselessly around their targets. This small artwork, then, seems to imply time and to manifest a sophisticated use of narrative, expanding the story beyond what is shown and making the viewer mentally fill in the rest. Could it convey a social commentary on the ineptness of lordly hunters who mostly miss their marks?

In contrast to these clever uses of art, the deer themselves, fatally hit, express emotion only through their wide eyes and lolling tongues. Death appears to be stylized, like bloodless bullet wounds in 1950s television westerns. Our distance from the Moche in time and space leaves open the question of how the maker and owner of a vessel like this actually read the depicted scenes. (98540012. Mark Craig, photographer.)

PLATE 6

Stirrup-spout bottle depicting
an owl
46-77-30/5031
Chicama Valley, Hacienda
Constancia, site of Mocollope
Moche, Phase IV
Earthenware, red and white paints
Width 14 cm, height 21.5 cm

THE SPOUT HAS BROKEN OFF the stirrup portion of this vessel, which takes the form of the head of an owl. Although it is stylized, the bird is likely a burrowing owl (*Athene cunicularia*), which is brown and white and distinctive in its round head and lack of ear tufts. The owl appears frequently in Moche art and is commonly shown as a warrior or priest. Because owls eat mice and rodents that threaten grain supplies, humans would have considered these birds friends, whether natural or supernatural. Trees are scarce in coastal Peru, and this owl has adapted by burrowing dens in soft earth, including abandoned adobe huacas and other structures. Because of the owl's link to the old huacas, Moche people likely associated it symbolically with ancestors. That it is active at dusk, dawn, and occasionally nighttime would have added to its supernatural aura, as would its habit of burrowing for prolonged nesting during March or April, the South American autumn, a season of transition.

A number of ideas, then, are conflated in the owl: ancestors, burials, huacas, night, underground, priests, and warriors. The warrior owl became a prominent figure in late northern Moche fine-line painted ceramics. It might even have been a newly emerged deity or one that previously played a minor role but became more prominent during the turbulent times at the end of the Moche era. (98540006. Mark Craig, photographer.)

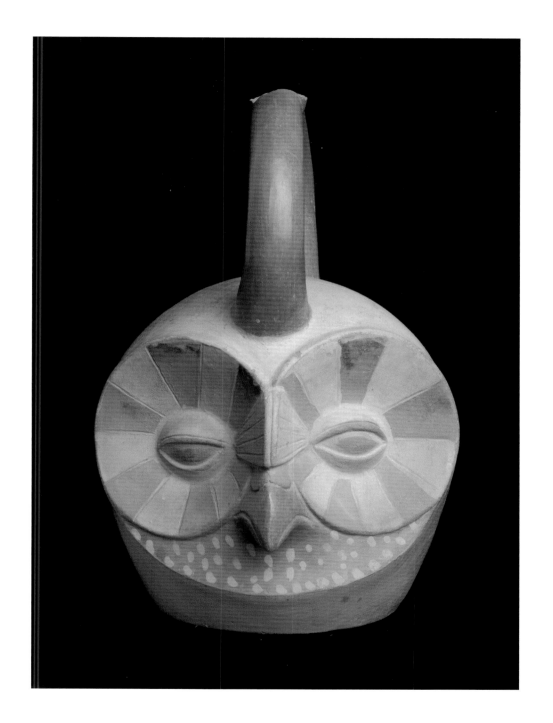

PLATE 7
Stirrup-spout bottle depicting
a feline-headed snake
46-77-30/5065
Chicama Valley, Hacienda Cartavio
Moche, Phase IV
Earthenware, red and white paints
Width 19 cm, height 26.5 cm,
length 14.2 cm

ALTHOUGH SOME ANIMALS appear completely natural in their Moche representation, the "feline-headed snake" is not one of them. It appears frequently in Moche art, often by itself, perhaps as an emblem for a political or ethnic group or symbolic of the supernatural realm. The body is clearly serpentine, but the facial features are difficult to interpret. It is possible that the head is not simply feline but combines the traits of a number of animals, such as the desert fox or a dog with fangs that cause it to resemble a serpent or reptile more than a mammal.

At Huaca de la Luna, a bas-relief of an immense but somewhat similar snake monster fills the triangular access ramp on the upper levels of the huaca, perhaps expressing the creature's role as an intermediary between cosmic realms. Another such creature, but two-headed and with arms, consuming dark-colored, cone-shaped objects, serves as a dividing line between two horizontal scenes in one of the more elaborate versions of the Presentation Theme, or Sacrifice Ceremony (see illustration on p. 53). This bicephalic version might represent the "ground" of a celestial realm. In other examples of this image, especially later in Peruvian prehistory, the two-headed serpent is often shown arched over anthropomorphic figures like a rainbow, with links to water and liquids in general. These ideas may stray far from the symbolism of the snake shown in this vessel, which gives the impression of being a fierce, dangerous creature. Still, the similarities among the images show both the complexity of pre-Hispanic Andean symbolism and the ways in which images and, likely, their symbolic content changed over time and across space. (98540005. Mark Craig, photographer.)

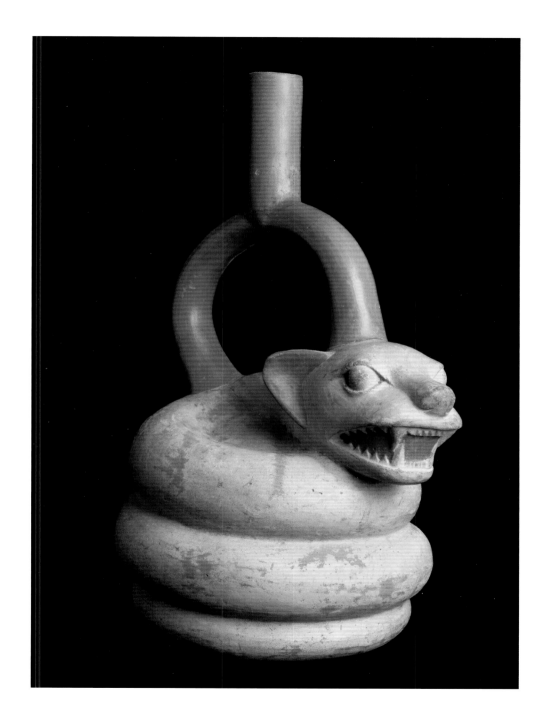

PLATE 8

Jar depicting stirrup-spout pots
09-3-30/75622.6
Department of La Libertad
Moche, Phase III
Earthenware, red and white paints
Width 14.5 cm, height 32 cm

THIS LARGE JAR EXPRESSES the value that Moche people placed on stirrup-spout vessels. Its primary motifs are bas-relief depictions of stirrup-spout pots and painted serpents arranged in panels created by vertical raised bands.

The size of the jar suggests that it was used to serve chicha, the fermented maize beverage that people almost certainly drank to excess during festivals, or possibly to receive the drink as an offering during funeral ceremonies. Perhaps the stirrup-spout decorations imparted to such festivities a sense of wealth and luxury, and the serpents connoted a supernatural world to be reached through inebriation. For the Inca and their descendants, the *amaru,* or rainbow serpent, was the bringer of water. The water of irrigated fields, the blood of human sacrifices, and the chicha of ceremonial feasting were symbolically linked as similar potent liquid forces. The wave scroll below the rim of this vessel further linked the liquid it held to Mamacocha, the mother sea.

The large size of this vessel and its elaborate decoration indicate that someone put considerable effort into making it. Although the snakes display relatively quick and free execution, the addition of the vertical bands and stirrup-spout vessels in bas-relief required an extra step that could have been eliminated by simply painting these images on the jar. Yet despite all this attention, the jar is lopsided and stands on its own only tentatively, suggesting that its functionality was less important than its appearance. Although the messages on the vessel are apparently simple, expressing liquid abundance, they are large enough to have been readable from fairly far away. If the jar was used in a funeral ceremony or as a receptacle for offerings in a tomb, then perhaps its stability counted for less than its message. (Opposite: 98540065; left: 98540066. Mark Craig, photographer.)

PLATE 9

Metalworking die
983-22-30/10989
North coast
Moche, date or phase uncertain
Copper-lead alloy
Width 2.8 cm, depth 1.6 cm,
height 5.8 cm

THIS SMALL METAL DIE WAS CAST in bronze, likely an alloy of copper and arsenic. Both ends of the bar depict a grimacing god face with double ear spools and a headdress with a fanlike crest, suggesting that the character is Aipaec or a similar deity as seen in the murals at Huaca de la Luna. The face also resembles that of the deity on a gilded copper bell from Tomb 1 at Sipán. An artisan would have pressed gold foil over the ends of the die to produce pendants or beads that could be strung on a necklace, such as adornments found with high-status burials at Sipán.

Although metalworking had been known in the Andes for more than a thousand years before Moche times, the Moche seem to have greatly increased the production of metal objects. Previous metalworking, such as that by Chavín artisans, appears to have been done individually, each piece separately crafted. The Moche, who employed molds so effectively to make multiples of ceramics, used the same ideas and techniques in metallurgy, as this die testifies.

Was the placement of two heads on a single bar an expression of dualism or merely the efficient use of metal? This piece exemplifies the integration of ideology and technology. A comparable modern example—on an admittedly grander scale—is the twentieth-century space race, in which the ideology of being first on the moon and the technical skills to achieve the goal were similarly intertwined. (Opposite: 98540025. Mark Craig, photographer.)

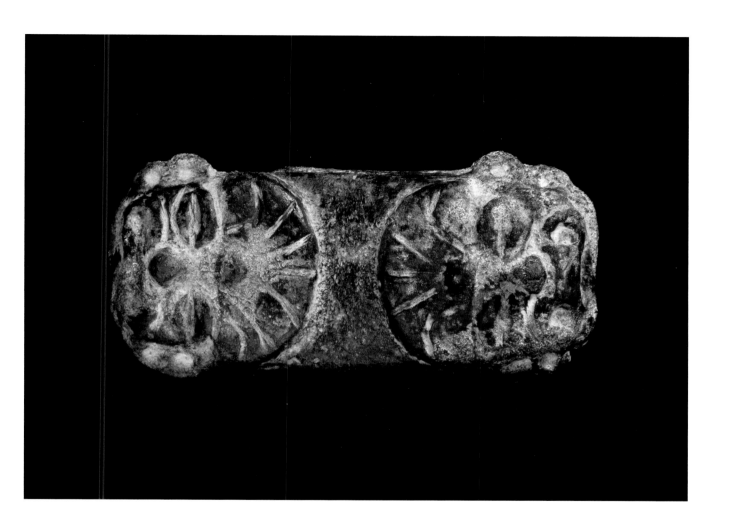

PLATE 10

Slit tapestry mantle border
(fragment)
42-12-30/3589
Tiwanaku
Moche, phase uncertain
Camelid wool (probably
alpaca) and cotton
Width 10.4 cm, depth 1.6 cm,
length 102.5 cm

MOCHE TEXTILES ARE RARE, possibly because drenchings from El Niño rains and occasional local showers from February through March aided their disintegration. Judging from the few textiles that are preserved, this fragment might have been an edging on a funeral shroud. An edging of similar dimensions, although different in design, was recently found on the border of one of the funeral shrouds of the woman known as the Señora de Cao, at Huaca Cao Viejo.

Two shades of pink-red yarns appear in the piece, as well as light brown, yellow, blue, black, and white. The image is that of a front-facing deity holding a long object in either hand, a deity form employed for many years by the ancient peoples of Peru, including the Moche. Here, the figure holds two long staffs with frets or steps. In Moche art he is more often shown holding two undulating snakes, as seen in a mural at Huaca de la Luna.

The "Staff God" is generally seen as a distinctly Middle Horizon phenomenon, associated with the great ceremonial centers and cities of Tiwanaku, in Bolivia, and Huari, in the south-central Peruvian highlands. His appearance on this textile may indicate that the piece dates relatively late in the Moche era. (Opposite: 98540022; below: 98540080. Mark Craig, photographer.)

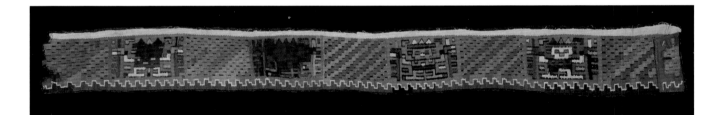

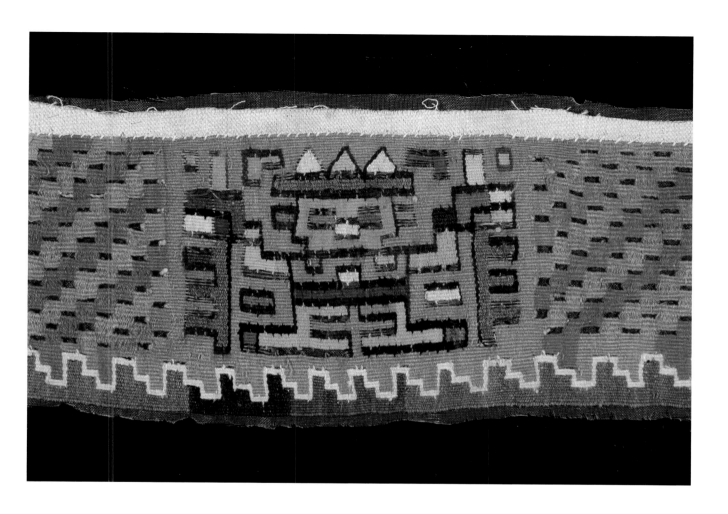

PLATE 11

Portrait head stirrup-spout bottle
46-77-30/5050
Chicama Valley, Casa Grande,
Hacienda La Constancia
Moche, Phase IV
Earthenware, red and white paints
Width 16.5 cm, height 29.5 cm,
depth 19 cm

THIS PORTRAIT HEAD VESSEL depicts the sensitive face of a relatively young person. Face paint in two broad bands of red runs over his eyes and down his cheeks. His headpiece consists of a large cloth that encases most of his hair, with sidelocks covering his ears. Layered over the cloth and tied at the back is a decorated band with serrated edges.

On the edge of the man's upper left lip is a distinctive, wishbone–shaped scar. Christopher Donnan has identified many portrait head vessels with such scars as representing a character he named Cut Lip.[58] Portraits of Cut Lip are known in which he ranges in age from about 10 to his mid–thirties. Most vessels also show two parallel scars slightly higher above the right lip.

The Peabody Museum's Cut Lip is a portrait of this man in his early twenties. In other ceramics that show Cut Lip advanced in age, he is depicted with two parallel lines that replace the wishbone scar, as if it has partially healed. The older Cut Lip also sports large ear ornaments (or large holes in his earlobes where they would have been placed) and distinctive black face decorations over his broad vertical bands. (Opposite: 98540069; left: 98540070. Mark Craig, photographer.)

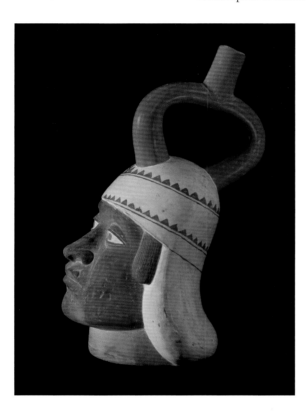

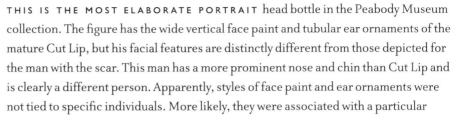

Portrait head stirrup-spout bottle
16-62-30/F729
Virú or Chicama Valley
Moche, Phase IV
Earthenware, red and white paints
Width 19 cm, height 35.5 cm,
depth 19.5 cm

THIS IS THE MOST ELABORATE PORTRAIT head bottle in the Peabody Museum collection. The figure has the wide vertical face paint and tubular ear ornaments of the mature Cut Lip, but his facial features are distinctly different from those depicted for the man with the scar. This man has a more prominent nose and chin than Cut Lip and is clearly a different person. Apparently, styles of face paint and ear ornaments were not tied to specific individuals. More likely, they were associated with a particular social role or status. Rod or tubular ear ornaments of the sort this man wears appear to have been the most basic Moche ear–wear and likely were made of a variety of materials, such as wood, cane, and bone. Gold examples have been found, too. Presumably, higher–ranking men wore ear rods of higher–quality materials.

Over the head cloth that encases his hair, this figure wears an elaborate hat or composite headpiece decorated with stylized birds and wave motifs. The back of the portrait is painted with an elaborate series of cloth bands that appear to hang vertically from the central band of the hat or headdress. The significance of the large mushroomlike object in the center of the headdress is unknown. On other portrait vessels, similar objects sometimes protrude from the headdress, singly or in pairs, on either side of the head. Whether these represent actual ornaments or indicate the status or state of the person portrayed is uncertain. They may represent the heads of stylized war clubs. (Opposite: 98540067; left: 98540036. Mark Craig, photographer.)

PLATE 13

Stirrup-spout bottle depicting
a headdress
09-3-30/75626.2
Chicama Valley
Moche, Phase III
Earthenware, red and white paints
Width 26 cm, height 23.5 cm,
depth 15 cm

THE IMPORTANCE OF HEAD COVERINGS in Moche culture is highlighted by this vessel, which itself depicts a headdress. This type of headgear is shown in Moche paintings on warriors in combat, so it might have been specifically associated with them. Each circle on the central part of the headdress has a small dark dot near the top, indicating that the designs represent metal disks attached to the headdress. In the illustration at left, a figure from a fine-line painting on a Moche bottle, a warrior wears a similar headdress featuring two pairs of arms and hands.

Outstretched and upraised arms and hands are commonly shown on gods in Moche art and may symbolize supernatural power. The depiction of the hands on the headpiece might refer to body parts cut off of rival combatants or sacrificial prisoners, or they could have some more abstract symbolism. On a warrior, they might have served to distract an opponent or to convey a sense of martial prowess, as if the soldier were carrying trophies of previous victims.

The Moche, like many other ancient Americans, conceived of a world without a sharp division between what we consider animate beings and inanimate things. The headdress, and this pot as well, might have played with the idea of the potential vitality of a headpiece. Jangling and flashing disks would have lent the headdress animation as its wearer charged into battle.

The stirrup spout on this vessel may not be original. Looters often combine parts from different vessels to make one more attractive to sell. The general form, however, appears to conform to Phase III of the Larco pottery sequence. (Opposite: 98540004; Mark Craig, photographer; drawing by Donna McClelland reproduced with modification courtesy of her estate.)

PLATE 14

Stirrup-spout bottle depicting
a puma attacking a prisoner
16-62-30/F727
Virú or Chicama Valley
Moche, Phase IV
Earthenware, red and white paints
Width 21 cm, height 27 cm,
depth 19 cm

THIS BEAUTIFULLY CRAFTED VESSEL depicts a feline, apparently a puma, attacking a bound, naked prisoner. We have no evidence that prisoners were tied and left in the wilds to be attacked by animals, and if such practices did take place, they would be extremely difficult to detect archaeologically. It might be, however, that the imagery is a metaphor for the sacrifice of prisoners by victorious warriors.

The depiction of prisoners is common in Moche art, and figurines of bound, seated prisoners are well known. This vessel is unusual, however, in showing the fate of such a victim. Curiously, although the prisoner's hands are tied, his feet are not, suggesting that he might have attempted to flee from the attack. This feature is a clue that the image is symbolic rather than a portrayal of an actual event.

The cross painted on the prisoner's face is a motif seen occasionally on Moche images, including those of deities (see pl. 24). Here, it may indicate the special status of the sacrificial prisoner. The prisoner also displays a hairstyle that includes a foreknot or some kind of hat. The deity depicted in the vessel in plate 24 has flares over his eyes that might be interpreted as a hat or perhaps exaggerated eyebrows. In either case, it appears that the details of the prisoner in the deadly embrace of the puma and those of the deity in plate 24 are related, suggesting either that the victim was designated a god impersonator, if the rite was actually carried out, or that the scene shown here is part of a myth in which a god is sacrificed to a feline.

At Huaca de La Luna, a small, windowless room adjacent to patios and plazas filled with the remains of sacrificial victims might have been used as a jail for prisoners before their demise. The exterior walls of this building, shown at left, are decorated with a poorly preserved frieze of felines attacking and killing humans.[59] (Opposite: 98540013; Mark Craig, photographer; left: Jeffrey Quilter, photographer.)

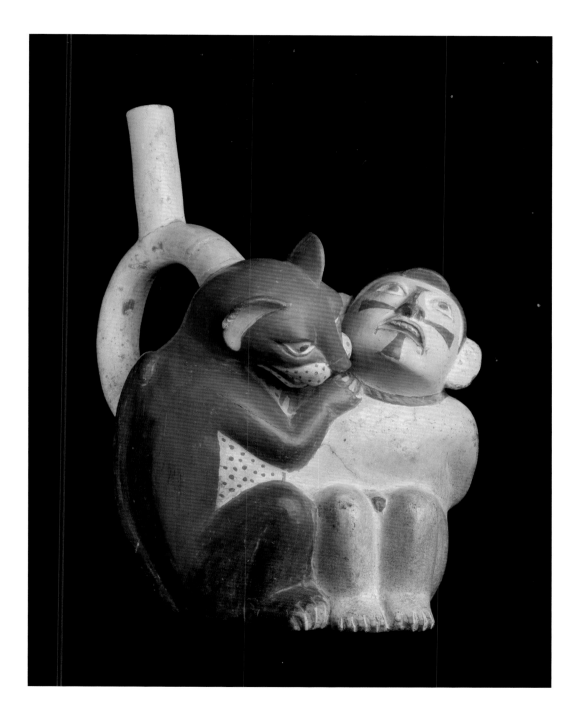

PLATE 15
Stirrup-spout bottle depicting
a prisoner
46-77-30/4980
Chicama Valley, Hacienda Sausal
Moche, Phase IV
Earthenware, burnished
Width 18 cm, height 19.5 cm

IMAGES OF SEATED PRISONERS like the one depicted here are fairly common in Moche art. This man has been deprived of his ear spools, other regalia, and clothing, except for a simple cloth head covering. He seems placid, either unaware or accepting of his grisly fate of torture and death. The rope around his neck seems more symbolic than the depiction of a real restraint. The figure lacks ropes not only around his feet but, unlike the prisoner shown in plate 14, also around his hands.

If this bottle was meant to serve as a substitute for a real prisoner, perhaps in a tomb, then such details might have been unnecessary. Moreover, perhaps not all prisoners were tortured and sacrificed. Maybe the man depicted here was of sufficiently high rank that he would be spared. But unless archaeological data are found to confirm or disprove such ideas, they remain simply speculations.

Black wares are relatively uncommon for the Moche; archaeologists usually think of them as emblematic of the subsequent Lambayeque and Chimú cultures. But artists made black wares throughout the Moche era, and they are among the finest of Moche ceramics. Possibly they were produced at a particular workshop, but because we lack detailed information about the places of origin of so many Moche pots, this remains yet another speculation for the moment. (98540040. Mark Craig, photographer.)

PLATE 16
Stirrup-spout bottle depicting
anthropomorphic creatures
16-62-30/F723
Virú or Chicama Valley
Moche, Phase IV
Earthenware, red and white paints
Width 15.5 cm, height 23.7 cm,
depth 20 cm

THIS VESSEL IS ONE OF THE MOST UNUSUAL and elaborate examples of Moche ceramic art in the Peabody Museum collection. The scene depicts a gathering of anthropomorphic creatures. The facial characteristics of the small figures and the spots on their bodies suggest that they may be fawns. Fully clothed and wearing an elaborate headdress, the largest, high-status individual might be a full-grown deer, although large fangs indicate that it is a supernatural with features that go beyond those of a simple deer. Five smaller figures are seated symmetrically around the main character, and the central figure among the secondary ones is larger than the other four. It and the two figures to its left hold covered bowls.

The scene takes place in a mountain setting. *Wilka* trees (*Anadenathera colubrina*) are painted on the lower part of the vessel. Moche people made the seeds of this tree into a hallucinogenic snuff. Perhaps the scene represents humans under the influence of this drug, transformed into deer, or deer in a supernatural realm behaving like humans. (98540021. Mark Craig, photographer.)

PLATE 17

Stirrup-spout bottle depicting
a recumbent male
09-3-30/75621
Virú Valley
Moche, Phase IV
Earthenware, red and white paints
Width 47.5 cm, height 26.5 cm

ONE OF THE LARGEST AND MOST UNUSUAL Moche vessels in the Peabody collection, this object's wide spout is the erect penis of a recumbent male. In the Chicama Valley, vessels with large, wide spouts have been found buried under floors at Huaca Cao Viejo, their spouts protruding through the floor surface. One example was a large owl head, generally similar to the vessel shown in plate 6 but less carefully rendered. A spout of almost identical form (though not representing a penis) protruded from the center of its head. Liquids, probably chicha, apparently were poured into these vessels as offerings to nearby burials. This bottle may have served a similar purpose.

Fangs identify the figure as a supernatural. He wears nothing but a headdress, and he holds the base of his penis as if to emphasize its potency. An animate penis conveys bodily fluids from internal space outward; this clay penis, in a mortuary context, serves as a conveyor from the outside world to an internal, perhaps subterranean one. As a god, this being might have been thought to emit power outward as well as to receive liquid offerings. These concepts of dualism, the flow of liquids, and inversion are part of a widespread Andean tradition.

White paint on the clay's red slip emphasizes the deity's eyes and fangs, features the Moche must have considered important. The shaft of the penis is similarly colored, and a white circle on the figure's chest might indicate a location of vital power. White paint was also applied in a circle at the top front of the headdress, above the vaguely rendered face of an animal or deity.

The maker also applied paint to the other end of the vessel, where the feet should be—but the piece shows no clear indication of feet, only bumps that suggest anklets, similar to protuberances above the hands that might be bracelets. In the tomb of the Lord of Sipán, a robust man was sacrificed and placed in a position suggesting that he guarded the other tomb occupants. His feet had been cut off, which archaeologists have interpreted as a way of preventing him from deserting his post. Perhaps the absence of feet on this figure kept the vessel deity in place. Lisa Trever has noted that the general shape of this object resembles a manioc tuber (see pl. 4), which might further explain the lack of feet. Multiple references to fertility may coincide in this vessel. (98540024. Mark Craig, photographer.)

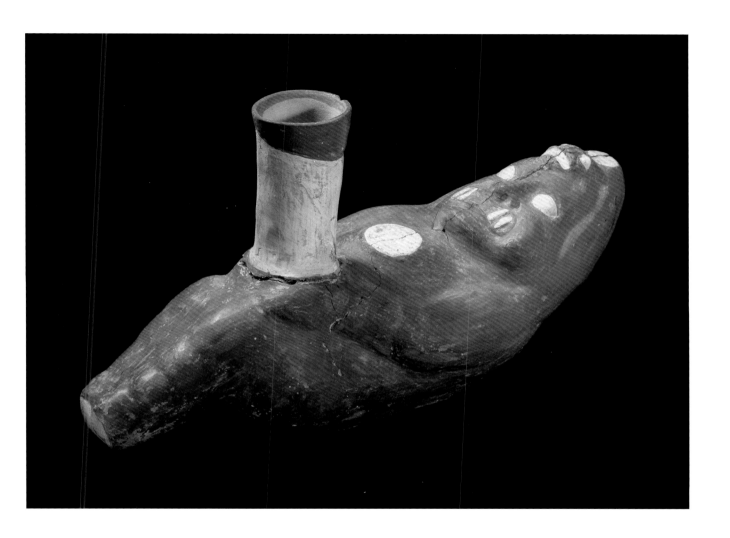

PLATE 18

Stirrup-spout bottle depicting
a danse macabre
46-77-30/5002
Chicama Valley, Hacienda Sausal
Moche, Phases III–IV
Earthenware, red and white paints
Width 11 cm, height 12 cm

ALTHOUGH THE STIRRUP SPOUT of this vessel is lost, its body is an elaborate depiction of a danse macabre. Comparing this scene with other known variants of it, we may identify the figures as the dead, holding hands in a dance in the afterlife. Smaller figures are shown playing instruments such as panpipes.

By itself, the inclusion of offerings such as food and sacrificial victims in graves indicates a Moche belief in an afterlife. This scene may express ideas about an underworld or perhaps even a "day of the dead." The dancers wear Moche warriors' costumes, and on the floor of the dance space appear bottles with ropes around their necks and distinctive mace–head stoppers. Because these bottles are linked symbolically to the Sacrifice Ceremony, the scene likely refers to an afterlife for warriors, perhaps those dispatched in sacrifice rituals.

Several other well–known Moche vessels depict scenes similar to this one— for example, the scene painted on the side of the vessel illustrated in plate 19. In all these cases the dead are shown as partial skeletons. Their bones are articulated, they wear headdresses and clothing, and they sometimes show other features suggesting that they retain sinews and some flesh. Often the figures are shown in a line, holding hands, which has led researchers to suggest that they are the dancing dead. Alternatively, the arrangement might represent the entrance of the recently deceased into the underworld.

The spectral quality of the images on this vessel was enhanced by the use of a shallow mold to produce the band of figures in low bas–relief, over which a wash of white paint created a ghostly scene. (98540046. Mark Craig, photographer.)

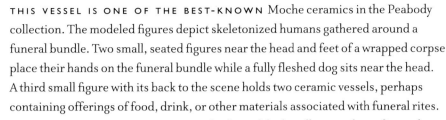

PLATE 19
Stirrup-spout bottle depicting
humans with a funeral bundle
16-62-30/F724
Virú or Chicama Valley
Moche, Phase IV
Earthenware, red and white paints
Width 23.5 cm, height 18.5 cm

THIS VESSEL IS ONE OF THE BEST-KNOWN Moche ceramics in the Peabody collection. The modeled figures depict skeletonized humans gathered around a funeral bundle. Two small, seated figures near the head and feet of a wrapped corpse place their hands on the funeral bundle while a fully fleshed dog sits near the head. A third small figure with its back to the scene holds two ceramic vessels, perhaps containing offerings of food, drink, or other materials associated with funeral rites.

At center, near the foot of the bundle, sits a large figure that apparently presides over the activities, with a small, partly opened box to its side. Painted around the sides of the vessel are skeletonized figures, some with penile erections. Most hold ceremonial war-club staffs. Smaller figures, perhaps children or juveniles, beat drums, and the figures with staffs appear to be dancing. The whole painting is reproduced in the "rollout" view shown below.

The scene can be interpreted as the reception of a deceased, high-status Moche person into the underworld. The large figure might be the Lord of the Dead or a high functionary in the afterlife.[60] In 2005, excavators discovered a funeral bundle at Huaca Cao Viejo similar to the one depicted here—the bundle encasing the remains of the Señora de Cao. For the first time, many details seen in this vessel were confirmed archaeologically. The stylized face painted on the bundle atop the bottle was matched by a stitched version on the funeral bundle shown at top left. (Opposite: 98540072; Mark Craig, photographer; left: Jeffrey Quilter, photographer; bottom: line drawing from Kutscher 1983: Abb. 162 reproduced courtesy Kommission für Archäologie Aussereuropäischer Kulturen des Deutschen Archäologischen Instituts.)

Stirrup-spout bottle depicting
a curing session
16-62-30/F728
Virú or Chicama Valley
Moche, Phase IV
Earthenware, red and white paints
Width 13.5 cm, height 21 cm

AMONG MOCHE SCHOLARS this vessel, too, is well known, and it has been discussed at length by a number of them, especially Christopher Donnan.[61] Eduardo Calderón, a modern–day curandero from the north coast of Peru, interpreted the scene depicted on the bottle as a healing session. A female curer, covered by a shawl, has been partly transformed into an owl, indicating that she is in a trancelike state. She holds what appears to be a slice of the hallucinogenic San

Pedro cactus, which Peruvian healers used to contact spirits. Calderón believed that the patient, lying next to the curer under a blanket, wore a mask of the deity Wrinkle Face as part of the cure. A painted helmet might be one that the sick man has removed in order to wear the mask.

Other materials similar or identical to those used in modern *curanderismo* are modeled and painted on the vessel. They include a box of cones of lime, used for purification; a bull-roarer, or noisemaker, used to attract or drive off spirits; and four strands of dried espingo (*Quararibea* spp.) seeds. These seeds come from tropical forests, have strong scents, and are used by curers for a variety of supernatural and other illnesses, as well as for offerings.

Although Calderón interpreted this vessel as representing the curing of a human being, another possibility is that the scene represents an event in a myth in which a god is cured of a sickness. Other scenes show what might be a sick or injured Wrinkle Face (see pl. 21), so this scene of his healing might have been part of a mythic cycle of stories. Because many examples of Moche art portray rituals carried out to reenact mythic events, it is possible that this vessel references both part of a mythic narrative and the practice of curing. (Opposite: 98540048; left: 98540049. Mark Craig, photographer.)

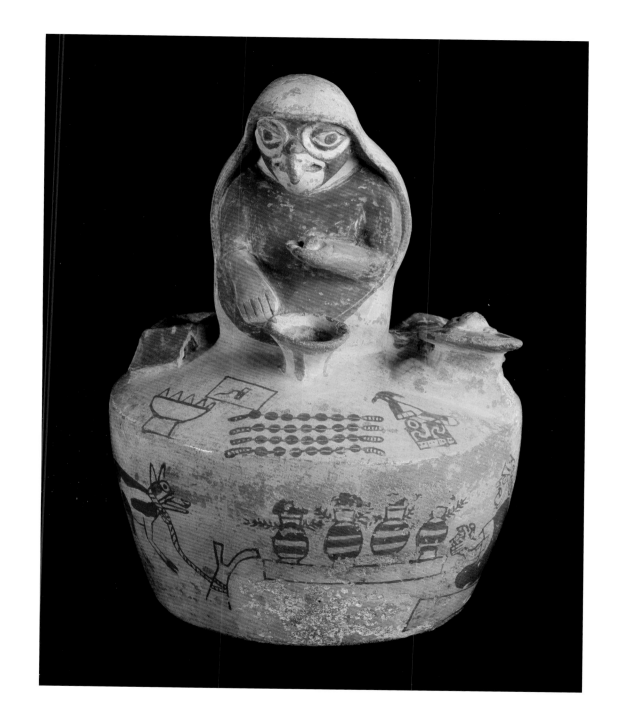

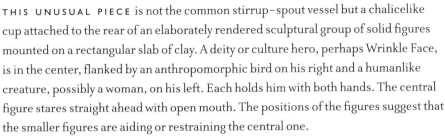

PLATE 21

Figural group with attached cup
16-62-30/F725
Virú or Chicama Valley
Moche, Phases I–II
Earthenware, red, white,
and black paints
Width (of base) 7.6 cm, height
14.6 cm, length (of base) 16.2 cm

Stirrup-spout vessel with
low-relief modeling
46-77-30/4949
Chicama Valley, Hacienda Sausal
Moche, phase unknown
Earthenware, molded figures in
relief, red and white paints
Width 11.8 cm, height 16.5 cm

THIS UNUSUAL PIECE is not the common stirrup-spout vessel but a chalicelike cup attached to the rear of an elaborately rendered sculptural group of solid figures mounted on a rectangular slab of clay. A deity or culture hero, perhaps Wrinkle Face, is in the center, flanked by an anthropomorphic bird on his right and a humanlike creature, possibly a woman, on his left. Each holds him with both hands. The central figure stares straight ahead with open mouth. The positions of the figures suggest that the smaller figures are aiding or restraining the central one.

Other examples of this vignette exist, including a molded and painted scene on a stirrup-spout bottle in the Peabody's collection (at left). In this second example, a bird and an iguana are the helpers, and a dog is added to the mix. These variations may be related to regional or temporal variations of myths.

The central figure in this version is dressed in the same regalia as that in the modeled piece and shows the same facial features, made more intense by an upturned visage. It is difficult to determine, however, whether the expression on the deity's face conveys the pain and suffering of someone being supported or dismay at being grabbed. A significant detail in the painted version is the depiction of one eye of the deity as smaller than the other, suggesting that the character is injured or in a trance, and therefore possibly that the other two are aiding him.

The cup on the back of the central figure in the piece opposite is painted with fine-line geometric decorations. Judging from a pair of similarly modeled and decorated figures in the Peabody collection (pl. 22), it seems likely that this assemblage had a near-identical twin. We might ask whether—if the god is indeed portrayed as wounded and aided by his sidekicks—the pair of cups was associated with curing rituals. (Opposite: 98540003; inset: 98540001; left: 98540033. Mark Craig, photographer.)

PLATE 22
Paired group of figures
with attached cup
16-62-30/F722
Virú or Chicama Valley
Moche, Phases I–II
Earthenware, red, white,
and black paints
Width of bases 8 cm; height
(left) 15 cm, (right) 14 cm;
length of bases 13 cm

THIS IS AN EXTREMELY UNUSUAL pair of vessels. Like the figural group in plate 21, these solid, modeled figures set on rectangular bases are a form rare in Moche ceramics. The conical shape and painted decoration of the cup on the back of the deity figure is also uncommon. All three objects likely came from the same workshop, possibly even from the same artist, suggesting that the cup shown in plate 21 was also one of a pair. Indeed, many Moche vessels were probably made as pairs, as were ceremonial drinking vessels among the Inca.

This pair is almost, but not quite, identical. The vessel on the left in the main photograph (A) is a centimeter taller than its partner (B). A also appears larger because the space between its two figures is greater; in B the woman's head nearly touches the deity's face. Although the gods are virtually the same height, A's torso is heftier than B's. In A, but not B, the woman's dress is decorated with dots in the middle of the circles. The carrying sling is the same on each, but the infant has white stripes across its shoulders in A and black stripes in B. Despite these minor differences, the themes depicted and details presented are true to Moche canons. Because the scenes portrayed here and in plate 21 are uncommon, they seem unlikely to be forgeries: We might expect a forger to depict more common themes.

The deity shown here has the distinctive cheek creases of Wrinkle Face and wears a double-headed snake belt placed behind him to add support and reduce the space taken up on the rectangular base (see inset). These features are not odd, but the deity's apparent attack on a seated woman is. He grabs her hair with his left hand, holds a conch shell (possibly a *Strombus*) in his right, and kicks her. Anthropology teaches us that customs vary around the world, so what appears to be an act of aggression in one society might be something else in another, and such could be the case here. This may be no ordinary woman, but a supernatural being. The circles on her dress link her to later Moche representations of a female deity who was impersonated by living priestesses.

The scene appears to portray a god or culture hero acting out a mythic narrative. The snippet of the story shown here was likely linked to a longer tale, perhaps related to the scene of the incapacitated Wrinkle Face shown in plate 21. (Opposite: 98540053; inset: 98540054. Mark Craig, photographer.)

PLATE 23
Stirrup-spout bottle depicting
the Decapitator God
09-3-30/75626
Chicama Valley
Moche, Phase III
Earthenware, red and white paints
Width 13.5 cm, height 21 cm

THIS MOCHE VESSEL HAS A SIMPLY RENDERED Decapitator God painted on its sides; the image is redrawn below. He displays fangs and eccentric eyes and wears a crescent-shaped crest and a tunic with wave scroll and serrated designs. On the sides of his head appear double-spool ornaments. Typically, he holds in his right hand a crescent knife with a rope handle, and in his left, a severed head. The eight linear elements extending from his arms and body might be references to his association with spiders, commonly depicted in Moche art as fierce predators. They also might be rays signifying the god's divinity, a motif used in later Moche times for the Warrior Lord or Rayed Deity. Similar representations of this god are found in relatively early murals at Huaca Cao Viejo.

This simple depiction draws our attention to the key elements of the Decapitator God, at least in one place during one phase among the Moche. The face is the largest element in the painting, and its fangs, eyes, double ear spools, and headdress are emphasized. In an economy of painting, the wave motif on the chest of the deity's garment ties him succinctly to concepts of duality as well as to maritime references. The zigzag motif below it may symbolize mountains. Without great elaboration, the figure is tied symbolically to life and death, land and sea, the world of humans and the world of the gods. (Opposite: 98540009. Mark Craig, photographer; left: drawing of the Decapitator God from Kutscher 1983: Abb. 221, reproduced courtesy Kommission für Archäologie Aussereuropäischer Kulturen des Deutschen Archäologischen Instituts.)

PLATE 24
Stirrup-spout bottle depicting
a Moche deity
46-77-30/5064
Chicama Valley, Nazareño,
near town of Cartavio
Moche, Phase I or II
Earthenware, red and white paints
Width 13.5 cm, height 15 cm

THIS MODELED VESSEL OF A MOCHE DEITY has lost its spout. All the features of its face are exaggerated beyond the usual depictions, making this a powerful image. The modeling is particularly strong in the prominent fangs, broad nose, and holes in the double ear ornaments. Because this is an early Moche ceramic, it is significant that the deity portrayed has many of the key features maintained in later religious art, particularly the double ears or ear spools and the fangs. Other features, such as the cross, the eyebrowlike elements, and the cheek markings, appear not to have survived in later times. The continuity of some features of deities and the disappearance of others, as well as potential regional variations, make the identification of a Moche pantheon difficult, although scholars have made much progress in doing so in recent years.

The Maltese–style cross on the bridge of the figure's nose is seen in Moche art on some deities and sometimes on prisoners, such as the one being attacked by a puma in plate 14, where it covers his face. The figure shown here also sports extended eyebrows, highlighted with paint, that are similar to the extension over the brow of the prisoner in plate 14.

Maltese crosses appear in other contexts in Moche art. For example, the rollout drawing shown above, from a painted vase, depicts what may be a nighttime scene of elite Moche consuming coca. The shield in front of the second figure from the right is decorated with a Maltese–style cross. Perhaps the mark signified some kind of sacred status or ethnic or political association. Comparing representations of such symbols on different objects is one way in which scholars advance the study of Moche art. (Opposite: 98540011. Mark Craig, photographer; above: drawing by Donna McClelland reproduced courtesy of her estate.)

PLATE 25

Trumpet
46-77-30/5016
Chicama Valley, Hacienda Sausal
Moche, Phases IV–V
Earthenware, red and white paints
Width 15 cm, height 8 cm,
length 37 cm

MANY MOCHE RITUALS were carried out to the sounds of music. No stringed instruments existed in South America before the arrival of Europeans, but native Peruvians created dense soundscapes by using a variety of wind and percussion instruments, the latter including drums, rattles, and poles with rattles attached. These were used en masse for large ceremonies, but we also have examples of smaller ensembles, including paired panpipes, again reflecting the Andean interest in dualism.

The instruments most commonly portrayed in Moche art are drums, rattles, panpipes, flutes, and trumpets. Wind instruments were made of cane, wood, or ceramic, and elaborate metal trumpets are known for cultures centuries older than Moche.

Pottery trumpets were often curved, similar to French horns, to produce a relatively deep sound in a small instrument. This example takes a feline-snake form, with the bell of the instrument shaped as the head of the bellowing beast. Fairly precise tuning could have been achieved through the manufacture of standardized ceramic instruments, although the sonic blast might have been more important than tonal considerations. Much research on ancient Andean instruments remains to be done in regard to such matters. (Opposite: 98540076. Mark Craig, photographer.)

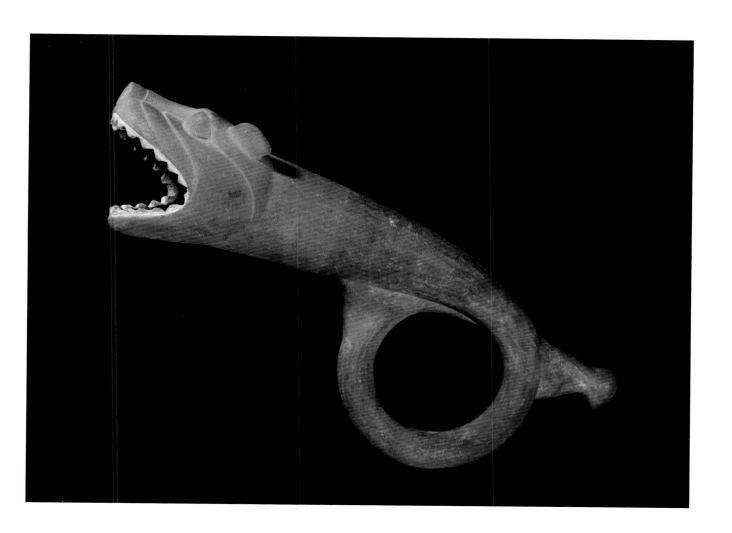

Notes

1. In the early colonial period, Muchik was spoken in the northern Moche region and Quingnam in the south, where the Moche Valley is located. The term *muchik* may refer to the middle of a river valley, traditionally seen as the best place to live.

2. Simon Martin, "On Pre-Columbian Narrative: Representation across the Word-Image Divide," in *A Pre-Columbian World,* edited by Jeffrey Quilter and Mary Miller (Washington, D.C.: Dumbarton Oaks Research Library and Collection, 2006), 55–106.

3. On Andean metallurgy, see Heather Lechtmann, "Cloth and Metal: The Culture of Technology," in *Andean Art at Dumbarton Oaks,* vol. 1, edited by Elizabeth Hill Boone (Washington, D.C.: Dumbarton Oaks Research Library and Collection, 1996), 33–44.

4. Susan Elizabeth Ramirez, *To Feed and Be Fed: The Cosmological Basis of Authority and Identity in the Andes* (Austin: University of Texas Press, 2005).

5. On the aesthetics of light in pre-Columbian America, see Nicholas J. Saunders, "Catching the Light: Technologies of Power and Enchantment in Pre-Columbian Goldworking," in *Gold and Power in Ancient Costa Rica, Panama, and Colombia,* edited by Jeffrey Quilter and John W. Hoopes (Washington, D.C.: Dumbarton Oaks Research Library and Collection, 2003), 13–47.

6. On the *warizo*, see Duccio Bonavia, *Los camelidos sudamericanos: Una introducción a su estudio* (Lima: Travaux de l'Institut Français d'Études Andines 93, 1996).

7. In Quechua, the Inca language, the word *huaca* is used for anything that we might call "sacred," although the concepts are not identical. *Huaca* is broader and more inclusive. Anything from a great snowcapped mountain to an idol in a temple, from the mummy of an ancestor to an unusually shaped potato, might be considered a huaca. On the north coast of Peru, the term has come to refer to the large adobe constructions that are commonly interpreted as having been temples or similar buildings.

8. For a general introduction to the archaeology and art of ancient Peru, see the books listed in the Suggested Reading section of this book. For general introductions to the Moche, see Garth Bawden, *The Moche* (Cambridge: Blackwell, 1996); Joanne Pillsbury, ed., *Moche Art and Archaeology in Ancient Peru* (Washington, D.C.: National Gallery of Art, 2001); and the introductory chapters in Izumi Shimada, *Pampa Grande and the Moche Culture* (Austin: University of Texas Press, 1994).

9. Thomas C. Patterson, "The Historical Development of a Coastal Andean Social Formation in Central Peru, 6000 to 500 B.C.," in *Investigations of the Andean Past: Papers from the First Annual Northeast Conference on Andean Archaeology and Ethnohistory,* edited by D. H. Sandweiss (Cornell University: Latin American Studies, 1983), 21–37.

10. Recently much attention has been focused on the site of Caral and similar large, stone-built complexes in the Supe Valley and nearby areas. Claims have been made for Caral as the earliest city and state in the New World. Further publication of the results of research at Caral is necessary before this claim can be fully evaluated. For a brief discussion of the debate on Caral's nature and importance, see "Showdown at the O.K. Caral," at the Discovery Channel website, http://discovermagazine.com/2005/sep/showdown-at-caral.

11. Richard Burger and Lucy Salazar-Burger, "The Second Season of Investigations at the Initial Period Center of Cardal, Peru," *Journal of Field Archaeology* 18, no. 3 (1991): 275–296.

12. On El Niño in Peru and elsewhere, see *El Niño, Catastrophism, and Culture Change in Ancient America,* edited by Daniel H. Sandweiss and Jeffrey Quilter (Washington, D.C.: Dumbarton Oaks Research Library and Collection, 2008). The degree to which El Niño events influenced culture change is difficult to assess, partly because the effects of the events are often localized, with devastating rains and floods in one valley but little precipitation in a neighboring one. Ultimately, it is probably not disasters themselves but social systems' strengths and flexibilities in recovering from disasters that determine when and how change occurred. See Brian R. Billman and Gary Huckleberry, "Deciphering the Politics of Prehistoric El Niño Events on the North Coast of Peru," in Sandweiss and Quilter, *El Niño, Catastrophism, and Culture Change.*

13. For a general discussion of the Late Preceramic Period, the Initial Period, and Chavín, see Richard L. Burger, *Chavín and the Origins of Andean Civilization* (London: Thames and Hudson, 1992).

14. For Huari, see the introductory sections in Gordon F. McEwan, *Pikillacta: The Wari Empire in Cuzco* (Iowa City: University of Iowa Press, 2005). For Tiwanaku, see John Janusek, *Ancient Tiwanaku* (Cambridge: Cambridge University Press, 2008); Margaret Young–Sánchez, ed., *Tiwanaku: Ancestors of the Inca* (Lincoln: University of Nebraska Press, 2004); and Alan L. Kolata, *Tiwanaku: Portrait of an Andean Civilization* (Cambridge, Mass.: Blackwell, 1993). For Chimor, see John H. Rowe, "The Kingdom of Chimor," *Acta Americana* 6:26–59.

15. The writings of some of the early Spaniards on the north coast are available in English and Spanish. For an English version of Cieza de León, see Clements R. Markham, ed., *The Travels of Pedro de Cieza de León, A.D. 1532–50, Contained in the First Part of His Chronicle of Peru* (Boston: Adamant Media, 2001). A second volume is also available from Adamant. Both volumes are facsimiles of the original English translation, edited by Markham in 1864 and published by the Hakluyt Society, London.

16. For a review of the history of Moche studies, see Luis Jaime Castillo B. and Jeffrey Quilter, "Many Moche Models: An Overview of Past and Current Theories and Research on Moche Political Organization," in *New Perspectives on Moche Political Organization,* edited by Jeffrey Quilter and Luis Jaime Castillo B. (Washington, D.C.: Dumbarton Oaks Research Library and Collections, 2010), 1–16.

17. Peruvianist archaeologists did not begin using radiocarbon dating routinely until the late 1960s, and even today it is not completely reliable by itself for building a chronology. Radiocarbon dates are reliable only within ranges of time; they are not precise. In addition, the date is for the material subjected to analysis, so that the reuse of old wood, for example, can bias the interpretation of artifacts or architecture with which it is associated. A suite of many dates taken from secure archaeological contexts and interpreted cautiously can be useful in building chronologies, but this requires a great deal of work.

18. The museum was originally housed in what might be called an art deco Moche building in the Chicama Valley. The remains of the structure and the local park, decorated in the same style, can still be seen in the town of Chiclín. In the 1960s the collections were moved to an old hacienda house on top of an ancient huaca in Pueblo Libre, which was then a suburb of Lima. The Rafael Larco Herrera Museum, named after Larco Hoyle's father, can still be visited today.

19. On the history of the Virú Valley Project, see the chapter on William Duncan Strong in Gordon R. Willey's *Portraits in American Archaeology: Remembrances of Some Distinguished Americanists* (Albuquerque: University of New Mexico Press, 1988), 77–96. On the research,

see William Duncan Strong, "Finding the Tomb of a Warrior-God," *National Geographic* 91, no. 4 (1947): 453–482; and William Duncan Strong and Clifford Evans Jr., *Cultural Stratigraphy in the Virú Valley, Northern Peru: The Formative and Florescent Epochs* (New York: Columbia University Press, 1952).

20. Garth Bawden, "Galindo: A Study of Cultural Transition during the Middle Horizon," in *Chan Chan: Andean Desert City,* edited by Michael E. Moseley and Kent C. Day (Albuquerque: University of New Mexico Press, 1982), 285–320; Christopher B. Donnan, *The Moche Occupation of the Santa Valley, Peru* (Berkeley: University of California Press, 1973); Christopher B. Donnan and Carol J. Mackey, *Ancient Burial Patterns of the Moche Valley, Peru* (Austin: University of Texas Press, 1978); Donald A. Proulx, *An Archaeological Survey of the Nepeña Valley, Perú* (Amherst: University of Massachusetts, 1968); Theresa Lange Topic, "The Early Intermediate Period and Its Legacy," in Moseley and Day, *Chan Chan,* 255–284.

21. Shimada's work is summarized in his *Pampa Grande and the Moche Culture.* For the English-language authors mentioned in this section, please see Suggested Readings. Other important works include the following: Yuri Berezkin, "Moche Society and Iconography," in *Pre-Columbian Collections in European Museums,* edited by Anne Marie Hocquenghem, P. Tamási, and C. Villain-Gandossi (Budapest: Akadémiai Kiado, 1987): 270–277; Yuri Berezkin, "Estructura social de la civilización Mochica y su reflejo en la iconografía [in Russian with a Spanish abstract]," in *Problemy arkheologii i drevnei istorii stran Latinskoi Ameriki,* edited by V. A. Bashilov (Moscow: Nauka, 1990), 223–247; Jürgen Golte, *Los dioses de Sipán: Las aventuras del Dios Quismique y su ayudante Murrup* (Lima: Instituto de Estudios Peruanos, 1993); Jürgen Golte, *Iconos y narraciones: La reconstrucción de una sequencia de imágenes Moche* (Lima: Instituto de Estudios Peruanos, 1994); Anne Marie Hocquenghem, "Les représentations de chamans dans l'iconographie mochica," *Ñawpa Pacha* (Berkeley, Calif.: Institute of Andean Studies) 15 (1987): 117–121; Anne Marie Hocquenghem, *Iconografía Mochica* (Lima: Pontificia Universidad Católica del Perú, Fondo Editorial, 1987); Gerdt Kutscher, *Chimu, eine altindianische Hochkultur* (Berlin: Verlag Gebr. Mann, 1950); and Gerdt Kutscher, "Iconographic Studies as an Aid in the Reconstruction of Early Chimu Civilization," in *Peruvian Archaeology: Selected Readings,* edited by John H. Rowe and Dorothy Menzel (Palo Alto, Calif.: Peek Publications, 1967), 115–122.

22. Walter Alva, *Sipán* (Lima: Backus y Johnston, 1994); Walter Alva and Christopher B. Donnan, *Royal Tombs of Sipán* (Los Angeles: Fowler Museum of Cultural History, UCLA, 1993).

23. Steve Bourget, "Rituals of Sacrifice: Its [*sic*] Practice at Huaca de la Luna and Its Representation in Moche Iconography," in Pillsbury, *Moche Art and Archaeology,* 89–109; Steve

Bourget, *Sex, Death, and Sacrifice in Moche Religion and Visual Culture* (Austin: University of Texas Press, 2006); Luis Jaime Castillo B., *La tumba de la sacerdotisa de San José de Moro* (Lima: Centro Cultural de la Pontificia Universidad Católica del Perú, 1996); Luis Jaime Castillo B., "The Last of the Mochicas: A View from the Jequetepeque Valley," in Pillsbury, *Moche Art and Archaeology,* 307–322; Claude Chapdelaine, "The Growing Power of a Moche Urban Class," in Pillsbury, *Moche Art and Archaeology,* 69–87; Christopher B. Donnan, *The Thematic Approach to Moche Iconography,* Journal of Latin American Lore 1, no. 2 (Los Angeles: Latin American Center, UCLA, 1975); Christopher B. Donnan, *Moche Art and Iconography* (Los Angeles: Latin American Center, UCLA, 1976); Christopher B. Donnan, *Moche Art of Peru: Pre-Columbian Symbolic Communication* (Los Angeles: Museum of Cultural History, UCLA, 1978); Christopher B. Donnan, *Moche Portraits from Ancient Peru* (Austin: University of Texas Press, 2004); Christopher B. Donnan and Donna McClelland, *Moche Fineline Painting: Its Evolution and Its Artists* (Los Angeles: Fowler Museum of Culture History, UCLA, 1999); Régulo Franco, César Gálvez, and Segundo Vásquez, "Los descubrimientos arqueológicos en la Huaca Cao Viejo, Complejo 'El Brujo,'" *Arkinka* (Lima) 1, no. 5 (1996): 82–94; Peter Kaulicke, "Moche, Vicús-Moche y el Mochica Temprano," *Bulletin de l'Institut Français d'Études Andines* (Lima) 21, no. 3 (1992): 853–903; Kristof Makowski, "La figura del 'oficiante' en la iconografía mochica: ¿Shamán o sacerdote?" in *En el nombre del señor: Shamanes, demonios y curanderos del norte del Perú,* edited by Luis Millones and Moisés Lemlij (Lima: Biblioteca Peruana de Psicoanálisis, 19 Seminario Interdisciplinario de Estudios Andinos, 1994), 52–101; Jean François Millarie, *Moche Burial Patterns: An Investigation into Prehistoric Social Structure,* BAR International Series 1066 (Oxford: Archaeopress, 2002); Jean François Millarie, "The Manipulation of Human Remains in Moche Society: Delayed Burials, Grave Reopening, and Secondary Offerings of Human Bones on the Peruvian North Coast," *Latin American Antiquity* 15, no. 4 (2004): 371–388; Santiago Uceda, Elías Mujica, and Ricardo Morales, eds., *Investigaciones en la Huaca de la Luna 1995* (Trujillo, Peru: Facultad de Ciencias Sociales, Universidad Nacional de La Libertad, 2001). Luis Jaime Castillo B. and Santiago Uceda also continue to issue yearly reports on their research.

24. Most Moche scholars believe that fancy pottery had some use in life. See Donnan and McClelland, *Moche Fineline Painting,* 19. Steve Bourget, however, believes that the majority of such vessels were used solely for burial offerings. See Bourget, *Sex, Death, and Sacrifice,* 49. As in other cases in Moche archaeology, I believe it is possible that during the long life of the style, uses shifted. Perhaps fancy ceramics played increasing roles as funeral offerings relatively late in the sequence.

25. Glenn S. Russell and Margaret A. Jackson, "Political Economy and Patronage at Cerro Mayal, Peru," in Pillsbury, *Moche Art and Archaeology*, 159–175.

26. On *tinkuy*, see Regina Harrison, *Signs, Songs, and Memory in the Andes: Translating Quechua Language and Culture* (Austin: University of Texas Press, 1989). On Andean dualism, see Richard L. Burger and Lucy Salazar-Burger, "Dual Organization in Early Andean Ceremonialism: A Comparative Perspective," in Luis Millones and Yuichi Onuki, eds., *El Mundo Andino* (Tokyo: University of Tokyo Press, 1993), 97–116; and Thomas F. B. Cummins, *Toasts with the Inca: Andean Abstraction and Colonial Images on Quero Vessels* (Ann Arbor: University of Michigan Press, 2002).

27. The variety of painted designs and other decorations suggests that diversity and novelty were part of what consumers of these vessels demanded. The implications of this for understanding Moche society are yet to be fully explored.

28. Investigating the aesthetic values of prehistoric people is difficult. For the Moche, my assessment is that objects in which greater energy was invested—those with more parts, more embellishments, and more care in their manufacture—were valued more highly than objects made more hurriedly. This is a subjective opinion and not a theory of aesthetics. The Moche might not even have had such a theory, but if they did, then perhaps the energy investment valuation was part of it.

29. The use of arranged figurines in burials of high-ranking people or as offering caches is found throughout the world at various times; many examples come from the tombs of ancient Egypt. In the New World, one of the best-known examples is an arrangement of stelae and humanlike jade figurines in an offering at the Olmec site of La Venta, Mexico. For details on the excavations at Sipán, see Alva, *Sipán;* and Alva and Donnan, *Royal Tombs of Sipán*.

30. Details on the pairs of vessels in the niche with the *Spondylus* shell have not been reported. Judging from available photographs (Alva and Donnan, *Royal Tombs of Sipán,* 120: fig. 129) and illustrations (Alva, *Sipán*), it appears that on the left side of the niche was a pair of frog or toad stirrup-spout vessels. On the right side were two seated human-figure stirrup spouts, one with the "mushroom cap" hat and the other with a conical hat or turban. The other vessel or vessels cannot be identified from the photograph; the illustration shows a single owl or other bird stirrup-spout vessel.

31. Recent research indicates that a variety of sacrifice rituals was performed, some of which were likely more open to a public audience than others. Here I offer an abbreviated version of one of them. Others were more elaborate. See chapters in Pillsbury, *Moche Art and Archaeology,* for discussions of these.

32. On the representational mode, or "verism," see Esther Pasztory, *Pre-Columbian Art* (Cambridge: Cambridge University Press, 1998), 129–143.

33. Alfred L. Kroeber, "Great Art Styles of Ancient South America," in Sol Tax, ed., *The Civilizations of Ancient America* (Chicago: University of Chicago Press, 1951), 207–215.

34. See Douglas Sharon, *Wizard of the Four Winds: A Shaman's Story* (New York: Free Press, 1978); and Douglas Sharon and Christopher B. Donnan, "Shamanism in Moche Iconography," in Christopher B. Donnan and C. William Clewlow Jr., eds., *Ethnoarchaeology* (Los Angeles: UCLA Institute of Archaeology, 1974), 49–77.

35. See Jeffrey Quilter, "The Moche Revolt of the Objects," *Latin American Antiquity* 1, no. 1 (1990): 42–65; and Jeffrey Quilter, "The Narrative Approach to Moche Iconography," *Latin American Antiquity* 8, no. 2 (1997): 113–133.

36. See Luis Jaime Castillo B., "Narrations in Moche Art," master's thesis, University of California, Los Angeles, 1991; Luis Jaime Castillo B., *La ceremónia del sacrificio: Batallas y muerte en el arte Mochica* (Lima: Museo Arqueológico Rafael Larco Herrera, 2000); Golte, *Los dioses de Sipán* and *Iconos y narraciones;* and Quilter, "Moche Revolt of the Objects" and "Narrative Approach to Moche Iconography."

37. There is a danger, of course, in circular reasoning—using interpretations from one set of data (art or archaeology) to interpret the other set and then later using the interpretations of the second set to reinforce the interpretations drawn from the first. This is a general problem in life as well as scholarship, and scholars, like others, should try to avoid it.

38. See Bourget, *Sex, Death, and Sacrifice.* Bourget's discussion of erotic scenes attempts to cover all such depictions throughout the entire corpus of Moche art. Although he argues that such art is connected to the life–death–ancestor transition, the weight of the evidence suggests to me that at least some of these acts were ritual sex performed by real victims, or perhaps mythological ones, about to be sacrificed. I believe sweeping generalizations about Moche art are best avoided. In this case, different kinds of sexual acts shown in Moche art may refer to different concepts expressed throughout the great geographical expanse and long duration of the Moche art style.

39. Susan Bergh, "Death and Renewal in Moche Phallic-Spouted Vessels," *RES* 24 (2003): 18–94. On sex and sex pots, see also Mary Weismantel, "Moche Sex Pots: Reproduction and Temporality in Ancient South America," *American Anthropologist* 106, no. 3 (2004): 495–505.

40. For a discussion of portrait vessels, see Bourget, "Rituals of Sacrifice," and Donnan, *Moche Portraits.*

41. The same is true today with what might be called modern demigods, such as Superman with his distinctive red cape, blue body suit, and heraldic *S* in a shield motif on his chest. So,

too, heroes such as George Washington are most commonly shown in standard clothing, not only of the times in which they lived or the political rank they held but also from within a limited range of all the apparel they wore. Washington and Abraham Lincoln are also most frequently portrayed at a distinctive age, usually older adulthood. These features make them more easily recognizable in art to viewers who know the visual cues that identify them.

42. A recent compilation of Muchik may be found in José Antonio Salas, *Diccionario Mochica-Castellano/Castellano-Mochica* (Lima: Universidad de San Martin de Porres, 2002). There, the word "Aipaec" is defined as "creator" (p. 1). See also Rafael Larco Hoyle, *Los Mochicas* (Lima: Museo Arqueológico Rafael Larco Herrera, 2001 [1940]), 267–350. Just as we cannot be sure that the Moche spoke Muchik, neither can we know whether the prehistoric image truly was that of a creator god.

43. To add further confusion to interpretation, sometimes artisans rendered figure-eight-shaped ears instead of ear spools. Whether these are two different ideas or whether, over time, artists misinterpreted ear spools for ears or vice versa is difficult to determine. For the present, I assume that whether depicted with ears or with ear spools, the god is the same, all other things being more or less equal, which indeed is the problem under discussion.

44. Degollador and Decapitator, even in cases when other aspects of their costumes, facial features, and so forth are consistent, are not always shown with double ear spools. Sometimes they wear large, hanging ear ornaments that resemble earrings. This underscores the point I am trying to make regarding the problem of variability of representation and the way it affects consistency in what or who is being represented.

45. Jürgen Golte, in *Los dioses de Sipán,* named the personage involved in these adventures (Wrinkle Face) "Quismique," and his assistant, "Murrup."

46. See Donnan and McClelland, *Moche Fineline Painting,* 65 (fig. 3.42), and Bourget, *Sex, Death, and Sacrifice,* 9 (fig 1.6).

47. Sherry Ortner, "On Key Symbols," *American Anthropologist* 74 (1973): 1338–1346.

48. Many people, particularly Roman Catholic clergy, denounced the superheroes of early comic books as fascistic, Nietzschian, pagan false gods. See David Hajdu, *The Ten-Cent Plague: The Great Comic-Book Scare and How It Changed America* (New York: Farrar, Straus and Giroux, 2008).

49. Donnan and McClelland, *Moche Fineline Painting,* 178–185.

50. I believe that although many supernatural creatures and activities are clear—monsters, for example—more ambiguity exists between many supernaturals and their activities than some scholars think.

51. Wendell C. Bennett, *The Gallinazo Group, Virú Valley, Peru* (New Haven, Conn.: Yale University Press, 1950).

52. See Elías Mujica Barreda, ed., *El Brujo: Huaca Cao, centro ceremonial Moche en el valle de Chicama / El Brujo: Huaca Cao, a Moche Ceremonial Center in the Chicama Valley* (Lima: ING Fundación Wiese, 2007).

53. Joanne Pillsbury, "The Thorny Oyster and the Origins of Empire: Implications of Recently Uncovered *Spondylus* Imagery from Chan Chan, Peru," *Latin American Antiquity* 7, no. 4 (1996): 313–340.

54. See Sharon, *Wizard of the Four Winds,* for a vivid account of contemporary shamanic curing sessions on the north coast.

55. There is some evidence that at Huaca de la Luna, the modeled figures were "refreshed" with paint and perhaps additional mud plaster at various times. How long each major phase in the growth of this huaca or any others lasted and what motivated a major building effort are key issues about which we currently know little.

56. See Thomas N. Bisson, *The Crisis of the Twelfth Century: Power, Lordship, and the Origins of European Government* (Princeton, N.J.: Princeton University Press, 2009).

57. See Donnan, *Moche Portraits,* 84–86.

58. Ibid., 140–159.

59. Santiago Uceda and Moisés Tufinio, "El complejo arquitectónico religioso Moche de Huaca de la Luna: Una aproximación a su dinánica ocupacional," in *Moche: Hacia el final del milenio. Actas del segundo coloquio sobre la cultura Moche (Trujillo, 1 al 7 de agosto de 1999),* edited by Santiago Uceda and Elias Mujica (Universidad Nacional de Trujillo and Pontificia Universidad Católica del Perú, 2003), vol. 2, 179–228.

60. See Bourget, *Sex, Death, and Sacrifice.*

61. See Donnan, *Moche Art and Iconography,* 95–100.

Suggested Reading

Publications on Moche have grown exponentially since the discovery of the Sipán tombs in 1987. Despite this, synthetic discussions are relatively rare, especially in English, and sources exist mostly as professional articles and books focused on specific themes. In many ways, three foundational books in English, published more than 30 years ago and now out of print, are still of value. They are *The Mochica, a Culture of Peru,* by Elizabeth P. Benson (New York: Thames and Hudson, 1972), *Moche Art and Iconography,* by Christopher B. Donnan (Los Angeles: UCLA Latin American Studies 33, 1976), and, also by Donnan, *Moche Art of Peru: Pre-Columbian Symbolic Communication* (Los Angeles: Museum of Cultural History, UCLA, 1978).

Benson's book covers Moche in general. Much of what she discusses is still accepted, although some particulars have changed. *Moche Art and Iconography* presents Donnan's research program for studying Moche art, including the use of ethnographic examples, archaeology, and the all-important thematic approach. *Moche Art of Peru* is an exhibition catalogue, but it provides plenty of text covering many of the points raised in Donnan's other book.

As of this writing, the most recently published monograph on the Moche is *The Moche,* by Garth Bawden (Cambridge, Mass.: Blackwell, 1996). It covers the environmental setting, everyday life, political organization, and symbols and rituals of power from early times to the

Moche collapse. Bawden is the first scholar to clearly attempt to view political organization and religion as separate but related on the north coast during the Moche era.

Christopher Donnan is not only the premier scholar of Moche culture but also a prolific writer. His books on Moche topics of interest to general readers as well as specialists include the following: *Moche Portraits from Ancient Peru* (Austin: University of Texas Press, 2003); *Moche Tombs at Dos Cabezas* (Los Angeles: Cotsen Institute of Archaeology, UCLA, 2008); with Donna McClelland, *Moche Fineline Painting: Its Evolution and Its Artists* (Los Angeles: Fowler Museum of Culture History, UCLA, 1999) and *Moche Fineline Painting from San José de Moro* (Los Angeles: Cotsen Institute of Archaeology, UCLA, 2007); and with Walter Alva, the catalogue for the Sipán exhibit, *Royal Tombs of Sipán* (Los Angeles: Fowler Museum of Culture History, UCLA, 1993). As the titles suggest, these volumes include discussions of ceramic traditions and coverage of fascinating and important excavations.

Steve Bourget recently published his summary view of Moche iconography, *Sex, Death, and Sacrifice in Moche Religion and Visual Culture* (Austin: University of Texas Press, 2006). With Kimberly L. Jones he edited a volume covering a range of topics: *The Art and Archaeology of the Moche: An Ancient Andean Society of the Peruvian North Coast* (Austin: University of Texas Press, 2008). *Moche Art and Archaeology in Ancient Peru,* edited by Joanne Pillsbury (Washington, D.C.: National Gallery of Art, 2001), is a set of chapters from a scholarly conference. The contributions mostly present good summaries of current knowledge about Moche in specific valleys, craft production, sacrificial rituals, and other topics. It is a fine source for readers who already have a general understanding of Moche. A recently published book that presents varying views of Moche political organization is *New Perspectives on Moche Political Organization,* edited by Jeffrey Quilter and Luis Jaime Castillo B. (Washington, D.C.: Dumbarton Oaks Research Library and Collections, 2010).

A large, richly illustrated book with texts in English and Spanish discusses the extensive research at Huaca Cao Viejo at the El Brujo archaeological complex: *El Brujo: Huaca Cao, centro ceremonial moche en el valle de Chicama/Huaca Cao, a Moche Ceremonial Center in the Chicama Valley,* edited by Elías Mujica Barreda (Lima: Fundación Wiese, 2007). A more scholarly treatment of a late Moche site complex is Izumi Shimada's *Pampa Grande and the Mochica Culture* (Austin: University of Texas Press, 1994). Besides looking specifically at Pampa Grande, Shimada includes a thorough introduction to Moche topics, including a review of previous studies, the environment, Andean culture history, and earlier Moche.

For readers of Spanish, the collected works of Rafael Larco Hoyle were recently published in a two-volume set, *Los Mochicas* (Lima: Museo Arqueológico Rafael Larco Herrera, 2001), which rapidly sold out its entire print run. We may hope for a reissue.

For readers interested in more general discussions of Peruvian prehistory, I recommend the following:

Berrin, Kathleen, editor

1997   *The Spirit of Ancient Peru: Treasures from the Museo Arqueológico Rafael Larco Herrera.*
        London: Thames and Hudson.
        This catalogue of some of the finest artifacts in the Larco Herrera Museum is much
        more than a set of pretty pictures. It includes articles by six leading scholars, mostly
        from the United States, and extensive discussions of the individual objects in the
        book. It serves as an introduction for novices and contributes new views for more
        advanced scholars.

Burger, Richard L.

1995   *Chavín and the Origins of Andean Civilization.* London: Thames and Hudson.
        A masterful text and many illustrations grace this book, which covers the archaeol-
        ogy and art of ancient Peru from the Preceramic period through Chavín. Burger's
        presentation is clear yet detailed. This is "required reading" for obtaining the
        equivalent of an advanced seminar in the early prehistory of Peru.

Lumbreras, Luis Guillermo, editor

2007   *Peru: Art from the Chavín to the Incas.* Paris: Paris Musées/SKIRA.
        This book illustrates artifacts from a large exhibition at the Petit Palais, Paris. Its
        essays, covering current knowledge and theories about the major archaeological
        cultures of Peru, are written by Peruvian and European scholars, including the edi-
        tor, the preeminent Peruvian scholar of Peruvian prehistory.

Moseley, Michael E.

2001   *The Incas and Their Ancestors* (revised edition). London: Thames and Hudson.
        This is a foundation document for studying the Andean past. Moseley begins with
        the Inca, the best-known Andean civilization, and then returns to prehistoric
        beginnings, covering Andean prehistory from earliest times through the eve of Inca
        expansion. Although the prose sometimes reads like a textbook, Moseley packs a
        tremendous amount of information into relatively few pages.

Quilter, Jeffrey

2005   *Treasures of the Andes: The Glories of Inca and Pre-Columbian South America.* London: Duncan Baird.

Despite its hyperbolic title, this book is filled with color photographs of Andean sites and artifacts from early prehistory to the Spanish conquest. The text is relatively brief, but it summarizes the key features of major cultures and the significant events of Andean prehistory for general readers.

Stone-Miller, Rebecca

2002   *The Art of the Andes: From Chavín to Inca* (second edition). London: Thames and Hudson.

Another essential book for beginning reading on the ancient Andes. Stone-Miller, an art historian, builds her discussion outward from exemplary objects, types of artifacts, and key archaeological sites to consider the cultures and ideas that produced them. Readers gain an understanding of the way arts and crafts developed in the contexts of changing social, political, and economic forces.